CHARLIE CHAPLIN

CHARLIE CHAPLIN

Maurice Bessy

with 1090 illustrations

HARPER & ROW, PUBLISHERS, New York
Cambridge, Philadelphia, San Francisco, London
Mexico City, São Paulo, Sydney

This work was first published in France under the
title CHARLIE CHAPLIN, © 1983 Éditions Pygmalion/
Gérard Watelet.

Translated by Jane Brenton

CHARLIE CHAPLIN

FIRST U.S. EDITION

Library of Congress Cataloging in Publication Data
Bessy, Maurice, 1910–
Charlie Chaplin.

Includes index.
1. Chaplin, Charlie, 1889–1977—Portraits, etc.
I. Title.
PN2287.C5B3813 1985 791.43'028'0924 84-43184
ISBN 0-06-015423-3

84 85 86 87 88 10 9 8 7 6 5 4 3 2 1

Contents

Wardrobe and accoutrements . . .

Introduction

There is an elusive quality about the film persona of Charlie Chaplin that defies explanation. The familiar jerky figure has the gestures and smiles of a man, but his gaze is that of an angel. You feel its magnetism and power. He might be a creature of the imagination, a character from your dreams who has somehow become superimposed on the everyday world. He is real and yet not real, a true creation of the phantom art that is the cinema.

Charles Chaplin, the man behind the persona, was born under the sign of Aries, and he possessed all the pride and enthusiasm associated with that sign, as well as a touch of the tyrannical and impetuous in his make-up. He led, as we know, a tumultuous life – and we recall that Aries is also the sign of conflict and contradictions.

With Chaplin, legend is already indistinguishable from fact. It's not merely the robbing of his grave that suggests the latter-day pharaoh.

But if his life has become a myth, one unchallengeable reality remains: the films he has left for posterity. Following a long eclipse, these have recently been enjoying a revival and are delighting new generations of fans.

This book is devoted to the reality, to the films that flickered across our cinema screens for half a century and are now being transferred with brilliant success to the small screen of television.

Cinema is the only art the twentieth century has created, and Chaplin was one of its most distinguished practitioners – indeed he embodied all the skills the cinema stood for, since he was screenwriter, director, actor, composer and producer all rolled into one. Individual creativity is paramount in film as in the other arts, and Chaplin stood alone in the completeness – the perfection – of his contribution.

For the first time a film-maker had invented a character who ranked with the great clowns of all time. But whereas the abilities of the others died with them, and we have no record of Tabarin or Mondor, Turlupin or Jodelet, Charlie Chaplin lives on, as the Tramp, the little fellow, Charlot, the Hobo – he has many names in many countries.

One wonders what future generations will make of those early slapstick films, in a poor state of preservation, much copied and edited, projected at breakneck speed, but nevertheless masterpieces of the imagination, brimming with invention and humour, and with their own logic and pathos. Essayists, critics and historians have already produced a multitude of studies and critical analyses of the phenomenon; there now exists a bibliography of such monumental proportions that it has been published as a catalogue in its own right – and even that is probably incomplete.

But films do not last for ever. Perhaps it is unrealistic to expect that the historians of the future will concern themselves with the nature of Chaplin's greatness. We live in a fast-changing world that is inimical to such old-fashioned scholarly assessments of the influence, direct and indirect, of this or that great man.

When the Middle Ages blossomed into the Renaissance it was at least in part due to the advances made by a small number of outstanding individuals, and until very recently their achievements conditioned the way people lived. But the twentieth century has ushered in 'modern times' with a vengeance, and our age is fundamentally different from everything that went before. Scientific, intellectual and social values are changing so rapidly and so radically that it would be foolish to deny that our world is undergoing a metamorphosis – and the speed of that transformation is not its least remarkable feature.

Does Chaplin have any continuing relevance in this process of upheaval and rebirth? Does he have a message for humanity?

As with all film, his life's work is essentially a series of images. Some of the most striking of these have been preserved in photographs, and occasionally film stills. These are the images we all remember.

This is as true of the 'minor' films as it is of his 'major' works. It is worth remembering that Chaplin himself was strongly aware of the power of the fixed image to attract audiences, and when he was shooting his big features encouraged the stills photographer to make as many exposures as possible. Paradoxically, the effect of this accumulation of visual records has been, in my view, not to diminish the classic shots, but to enhance them and give them the status of archetypes. Collected together as they are here, they powerfully evoke the richly imaginative fantasy and inventiveness of the originals. Stirring and pungent images in their own right, they are often intensely moving.

Moments of frozen time, they speak volumes.

They begin to function like hieroglyphs or ideograms, carrying both literal meaning and an underlying significance.

Alfred de Vigny once said: 'The foremost among men will always be those who make something enduring from a sheet of paper or a canvas, a block of marble or a sound.' Chaplin will perhaps be the first of the truly great whose legacy to the future is a cryptic trace of long-ago movement.

The photographic records assembled here are more than pictures to be looked at. They are documents to be read.

A First Encounter with Charlie Chaplin

There used to be an orphanage in the Saint-Jean area of Nice, occupying a house once owned by the King of Belgium. It was full, I remember, of laughing children. Most of them were still too young to understand what the war had done to them; it was only later, when they experienced life's problems, that realization of their predicament began to dawn.

They were dressed in drab uniforms and all looked alike. When I passed by, I used to catch sight of them through the bushes lining the fence.

One day I actually went inside. They were all assembled in a big wooden shelter. A number of benches had been placed in rows on the trampled ground, and at one end a sheet was stretched out on the wall, making a splash of white. The projector was set up in the middle of the area where we were sitting. It was an ancient machine that had to be cranked by hand and proceeded by violent fits and starts. A fat light bulb flickered inside a metal box, giving off a terrible smell as it overheated; sometimes its position had to be adjusted slightly when the shadow of the filament was cast onto the screen.

In these dismal surroundings a figure suddenly sprang to life who was like something out of a crazy dream. I shall never forget my first sight of that extraordinary apparition with his jerky gestures and flapping shoes.

The film was set in a bakery and the boss was a fat white-faced man with a fierce expression. There was a vast array of little pies, all neatly stacked, that would come tumbling down at just the right moment. Then the droll little man would fall into the vat of dough. The mixture clung to his clothes, and of course the more he struggled the deeper in difficulty he got.

In that old shed everything else simply melted away. Paying customers at twenty-five centimes a seat, war orphans, projectionist, all were forgotten. There was just an inhuman gale of laughter that filled the whole space, blotting out everything. A gigantic belly-laugh that racked us with violent convulsions. I was beside myself.

Suddenly the lights went on. We were bereft.

There was another film, a long one. It was called *Christus* and was about the life of Jesus Christ.

At first we all kept very quiet. Out of respect. There were crosses and the Virgin Mary and Joseph and handsome muscular soldiers. But soon it all began to seem very bleak and depressing. We knew the story by heart anyway, and of course there wasn't even any colour to liven it up, like the bright pictures in the church where we used to follow the stations of the cross.

But I don't think that was all. I suspect everyone there was thinking the same as I was. Every time a character appeared I tried putting in his place the little figure we had seen earlier. So even Jesus acquired a bowler hat and curly hair; Joseph a small black moustache; Pontius Pilate a worn frock-coat.

Suddenly I burst out laughing, shattering the silence. No one objected. By then we'd reached the Mount of Olives and I could picture him absolutely clearly, the man from the previous film, his feet sticking out, grabbing hold of his halo and eating it like a round loaf of bread. Again I exploded with laughter. One or two others followed suit. It was infectious, and soon everyone began to laugh and shout. I leapt on to my bench and cried:

'Vive Charlot!'

A hundred voices echoed in chorus:

'Vive Charlot!'

There was pandemonium. The shouts rang out: Charlot! Charlot! Charlot! Some of the children planted themselves in front of the projector and their big blue shadows effectively blotted out *Christus*.

'We want Charlot!'

The projectionist switched off and went to put on the lights. Removed *Christus* from his machine. Fetched the Chaplin film and held it up with a smile. It consisted of two black reels with a piece of celluloid sticking out at one end. But of course the film was now reversed, and he realized he had no winder.

No matter! he decided to re-wind on the projector, so we ended up seeing the film backwards.

Thus, in an extraordinary manoeuvre, we were able to see Charlot climbing out of the vat of dough, and actually making custard pies from the gooey mess on his fellow actors' faces.

We took it in turns to help the projectionist crank the handle; sometimes the person operating the machine was so overcome with giggles that he couldn't go on; then there would be a faint smell of burning and he'd hastily return to his task.

The orphan children literally wept with delight. I saw them sitting there when it was over, pink with pleasure. Only one looked sad, not all that sad, but a little downcast.

'Is there something wrong?'

He was taller than I and he had freckles on his face.

'No, it's just that my dad was a baker too.'

Charlie Stays the Night

The following anecdote was told by Chaplin. It may be true, or he may have made it up from various things that happened to him at different times. At all events it gave us pleasure to hear it, and the only cause for regret is that in the retelling it lacks Charlie's inimitable warmth and his perennially youthful enthusiasm.

It was during the Second World War, and Chaplin was travelling to New York. He arrived there at night and hadn't bothered to reserve a room in advance. The hotel where he normally stayed was full, so he hired a taxi and went to another hotel. Again no luck. For two whole hours the taxi drove round the city, but without success.

Tired from the journey and exhausted by all this driving about, Chaplin lapsed into a momentary depression. The driver stopped his cab, turned to his passenger, whom he had recognized, and made a proposal.

'Look, we can drive around the whole night if you want, but you still ain't going to get into any hotel in the whole of New York. There's only one thing for it: it's getting late and I'm making for home. It's no palace but it's OK. My wife's away and my boy's got a big bed. If you want to come home with me, the offer's there.'

Chaplin accepted, climbed into the front seat next to the driver, and they headed for Brooklyn. They chatted away like old friends, about the war, the blackout, the shortages.

It was a modest apartment, tiny and sparsely furnished but spotlessly clean and gleaming with polish, so that you completely forgot the stale smells on the staircase.

'We'll wake the kid,' said the taxi-driver.

The child was sleeping in a big brass bed, his teeth gritted and his brow furrowed with concentration, no doubt dreaming of heroic feats performed by Tarzan or the adventures of Blondie. He was a boy of about eight, dark-haired and pale-skinned; a boy like any other from a poor part of town, whether the docks of Naples, the slums of Ménilmontant in Paris or the Kennington Road in London. An undernourished little street urchin, with a first hint of a line appearing at the corner of his mouth.

'Mickey,' exclaimed the man. 'Look who I've brought to see you, it's Charlie Chaplin!'

The child woke up reluctantly. He was a good lad, a true poor man's son. He'd eaten his supper alone and gone to bed at the proper time, there wasn't much to look forward to except the dreams he had at night. The harsh lamplight made him blink.

'It's Charlie, I tell you, Charlie Chaplin.'

He thumped his pillow, reared right up and fell back on his bed. He looked at his white-haired visitor.

'Wow!'

It had to be a dream. He rubbed his eyes.

'You look like him,' he said, 'but you don't have a moustache. And he's got black hair.'

'Never mind about that,' the father cut in. 'If I say he's Charlie, then he's Charlie!'

Chaplin took off his coat and sat in the armchair. He was exhausted.

'I'm going to sleep in with you,' he smiled.

The child recognized the smile.

'It's a fact, you do look like him. But if you really are Charlie, go ahead, act like Charlie.'

He was wide awake now and brimming with anticipation. So

Chaplin stood up and improvised for his audience of one the pantomime of his dreams. He danced around the little bedroom, using the various objects as props, leaping on to chairs, slipping over, falling down, clutching on to the drapes.

'More, more,' cried the child in delight. 'You really are Charlie.'

Chaplin was no longer conscious of his tiredness. All he was aware of were those two eyes glued to his every move, every smile, every twist and turn of his clown's body. He twirled an imaginary cane, skidded to a halt on one foot . . .

We can imagine the scene, Charlie re-enacting his youth in a little room somewhere in Brooklyn. His old muscles suddenly taut; on his face the grin of the shabby urchin let loose in Hamisch Street; on his lips scraps of verse that might have been made up by an adolescent boy one autumn evening in Fitzroy Square:

A glass in my hand
In a peaceful land
In some old town
For that happy fate
I'm prepared to wait!

There he was, acrobat, mime, actor and dancer. The great Chaplin displaying all his talents, giving not a thought to fame or fortune or advancing years. For the moment nothing else mattered except the enchantment of one small boy, transfigured by happiness.

With a pirouette he stooped to open his case, undressed and put on his pyjamas. All as part of the dance. The child slipped into a happy, dreaming sleep in Chaplin's arms.

A true professional, Chaplin rounded off this admirable tale with an epilogue.

'You couldn't help thinking', he said, 'of what this boy would tell his friends at school the next day. He wouldn't be able to keep it to himself that Charlie Chaplin came to stay the night, that he went through his whole act just for him, and actually shared the same bed.

'And all the other boys would have burst out laughing. "Charlie Chaplin! Pull the other one! He's in Hollywood." "You think he'd come here just to see you . . . Liar, boaster."

'The sensible ones would have shaken their heads: "That kid lives in a world of his own. Either that or he dreamt it." "They say there's a cure for it."

'And he'd have been left standing alone in the schoolyard, his friends jeering and pouring scorn.

' "But it's the truth, honestly . . ." '

No, they'd never believe him. But it wouldn't matter. It might cast a cloud over his happiness, but he'd be smiling through his tears – like the tramp setting off on the open road. No one could take that feeling of joy away from him, the same elation we felt all those years ago in that bare courtyard, which was transformed for a while into a corner of paradise.

Left, forcing an entry into the world of music (*Police, 1916*)

Above and right, 'We are such stuff as dreams are made on' – William Shakespeare (*Sunnyside*, 1919)

1915, first signed photograph

Chaplin's father and mother

The parents of Charles Chaplin, Hannah Hill and Charles Chaplin, were both touring vaudeville performers.

Hannah Hill, born in 1867, sang under the name Lily Harley. She was the daughter of Charles Hill, an Irish cobbler from County Cork, and Mary Smith, described by Chaplin as a dancer and 'half-gypsy'. Hannah had fallen in love at a young age with one Sydney Hawkes, apparently a Jewish bookmaker, whom she had met while touring. They lived together in South Africa. She later claimed they were married, and a few weeks after her return to England on 16 March 1885, she bore him a son to whom she gave the first name of his father and her own maiden name, Hill. (It was not until much later that Sydney adopted the surname of his famous half-brother.)

Charles Chaplin senior had known Hannah before she went away to Africa, and married her in 1886 after her return.

Charles Spencer, known as Charlie, was born three years later, on 16 April 1889. His father left home two years after his son was born.

Hannah then lived with an actor named Leo Dryden, although it is unlikely that they married. She had two children by him, Guy and Wheeler, both of whom were acknowledged by Dryden as his.

Chaplin senior lived with another singer, called Louise, while contributing to the support of Hannah whose health broke when Charlie was five. His father assisted the theatrical début of the young Charlie Chaplin by proposing that the boy should join a clog-dancing troupe, the Eight Lancashire Lads.

At Kennington Road School, aged seven-and-a-half

Charlie, aged sixteen, appears (centre) as one of the Eight Lancashire Lads at Casey's Court Circus in London, 1905

Charlie (seated second from left) with Fred Karno's hockey team in Liverpool in 1909. Behind him, standing, is Arthur Stanley Jefferson, later known as Stan Laurel

Karno's company in London in 1908.
Charlie appears third from the left.
Arrowed: Stan Laurel

Fred Karno

Poster for the Karno tour of the United States, 1913. Charlie features twice

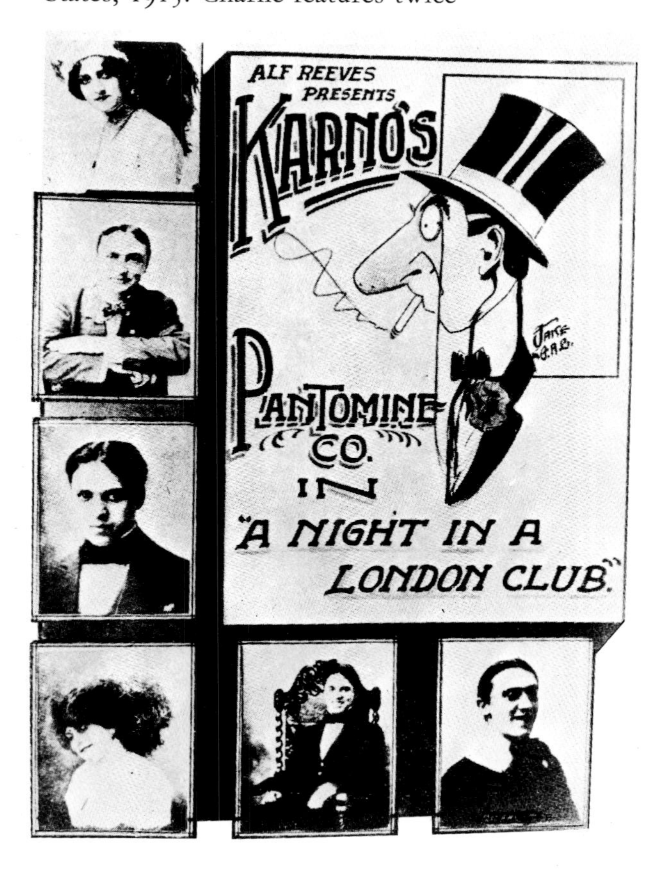

Fate beckons him to the New World . . .

To Hollywood

Fate beckons him to the New World – shades of *The Immigrant*. Chaplin arrived in the United States in 1910. Opposite, his rendition of a seasick passenger

Newly arrived in Hollywood, Chaplin recalls that at the age of sixteen he wore a moustache in a sketch called *Doctor Walford Bodie* (right); he accepts a day's work as an extra (centre), but (below) already poses for his first solo poster in 1914

The first tramp costume

A man's personality is as unique to himself as the perfume of a flower

Opposite, Chaplin appears in his first tramp costume. It was borrowed without qualms by his older half-brother, Sydney Hill, later Sydney Chaplin, who appears (below) with Phyllis Allen, Cecile Arnold and Slim Summerville in the long-forgotten *On Gussle's Day of Rest*. Sydney scored a notable success in *Charley's Aunt* (left)

Overleaf, at top, Jackie Coogan, star of *The Kid*, wearing his director's famous tramp costume in 1921

The early years

'In those early years of the cinema Chaplin was outstanding, in no small measure responsible for transforming an entertainment into an art. The roll-call of that era contains some illustrious actors' names . . . But where the rest gave performances, Chaplin gave us himself.'

Louis Delluc

The character of Charlie is not a comic character. His shabby clothes are those of a man who is down on his luck. The cane is a mark of elegance, even snobbishness. It is the sole remaining personal possession of this unfortunate fellow, and that is why he flourishes it with such pride . . .

Above, one of Hollywood's future great stars, Gloria Swanson, who played a tiny part in Chaplin's *His New Job* (1915)

Opposite, Hollywood's Three Musketeers: Douglas Fairbanks as Zorro, Mary Pickford in *Secrets* costume, Chaplin playing the violin left-handed

Above, George Bernard Shaw, the toast of Hollywood, with Chaplin, Marion Davies, Louis B. Mayer, Clark Gable. Shaw remained unimpressed . . .

Opposite page, top left, Chaplin with Francis X. Bushman, Ramon Novarro's rival in the silent *Ben Hur*, and Gilbert Anderson, one of America's most famous film actors, who played the first screen cowboy, Broncho Billy. Anderson also appeared in *The Great Train Robbery* in 1903, and was co-founder with George Spoor of the Essanay (S and A) Company. Top right, with Robert Florey, Marcel Achard and Bernard Zimmer in 1934. Centre left, with Marc Chadbourne, in 1934. Centre right, Chaplin in 1945 with Alf Reeves (1876–1946), former manager of the Fred Karno company, who worked closely with him until his death. Bottom, with the Scottish singer Harry Lauder on the set of *The Kid*

Right, the triumphant smile of a twenty-eight-year-old who has just signed a million-dollar contract (with First National in 1917). Having earned a mere $100 per week in 1914, Chaplin became one of the richest men in Hollywood

With Douglas Fairbanks . . .

Chaplin's colleague, companion and close friend

The great Swedish director (best known for *The Phantom Carriage*, 1920) appears with Chaplin in 1924

Time off

Chatting to Wilbur and Orville Wright (above), and (below) sparring with the tall boxer Primo Carnera

Jackie Coogan – the 'Kid' no more

From counterfeit gentleman to veritable tramp

The transformation was effected in Mack Sennett's dream factory, a place of catastrophes, pretty girls and acrobatic cops

Mack Sennett's strongest weapons

First, slapstick. Second, the Bathing Beauties (here seen with Chester Conklin)

Taking a dip, Sennett-style

Although he met a whole host of pretty girls at Keystone, Chaplin never asked any of them to be in his later films. Mack Swain and Gloria Swanson are among the group in the first photograph

'I knew practically no one in Los Angeles when I first arrived in California and I had a lot of trouble finding Mack Sennett's studio, since my taxi driver didn't know the suburbs of that city any better than I did. I arrived late, and Sennett had already left his office. Thinking I might find him on one of the sets, I strolled around the little studio, studying what was going on with curiosity. Working there at the time was Ford Sterling, whom I'd seen in films, and I was not a little surprised to see the grimaces with which he punctuated his work. Fred Mace I'd met backstage at the theatre where we played *A Night in a London Club*, and he introduced me to my future colleagues with the words: "Charlie Chaplin is the English comic who'll be acting with us." I looked for Mack Sennett for the rest of the afternoon, but without success, and finally returned to my hotel. One of the publicity men invited me to dinner and to spend the evening at a music hall in Main Street. In the interval he told me his boss was in the audience, and I went to introduce myself. "I waited more than an hour for you this morning," said Sennett, "then I had to go out on location to keep an eye on one of our companies . . ." We chatted for a few minutes and Sennett told me once again that I seemed very young to him, and he would be curious to see how I would turn out on film. The next day I arrived at the studios without a hitch, and Sennett asked me what I could do. "Anything and everything you want," I replied, but several weeks passed before I appeared in front of a camera. I did several tests but none of the directors seemed in any hurry to give me a part, finding my acting too different from the grotesque/burlesque style they were used to. It was by now around early January, and I was almost beginning to regret that I had left Fred Karno, but I still hadn't given up hope.'

Chaplin in conversation with Robert Florey

Mack Sennett's bathing beauties

The comic cops . . .

Among the actors (above) in the photograph of the Keystone cops (1913) are Ford Sterling, Al 'Fuzzy' St John, Edgar Kennedy and Roscoe 'Fatty' Arbuckle

Max Asher, a Dutch actor who joined the company in 1912, seen here with Alice Davenport (later to appear in Chaplin's first film *Making a Living*), in *After the Ball*

Three stars of 1913: Harold Lloyd, Bebe Daniels and Snub Pollard

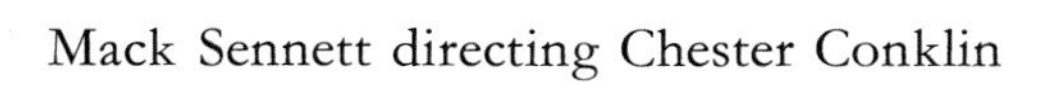

Mack Sennett directing Chester Conklin

Fatty Arbuckle starts his career as straight man to Jackson the clown (above), but by 1911 he is Mabel Normand's co-star

The art of the blunt instrument

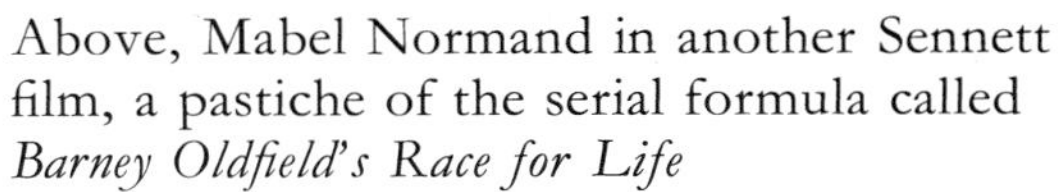

Above, Mabel Normand in another Sennett film, a pastiche of the serial formula called *Barney Oldfield's Race for Life*

Below, Fatty Arbuckle, Lew Fields, Joe Weber. The mallet so often wielded in Mack Sennett movies was a big hit with the public too. Chaplin tried his hand with it and came close to keeping it as a regular prop in preference to his cane

Humble beginnings for Charlie when he joined Sennett's studios

Above, the 'fun factory', and below, some of the employees: the Keystone Company in 1913. Roscoe 'Fatty' Arbuckle, Bobby Vernon and Mack Swain are easy to pick out. True fans may spot Al St John, Slim Summerville, Billy Armstrong, Henry 'Pathé' Lehrman, Eddie Cline, Victor Potel, Glen Cavender, George Jeske and Joe Bordeaux

Cartoon by Cami

'King of comedy' Mack Sennett

. . . and his queen Mabel Normand (1894–1930), who was Chaplin's first leading lady. Off the set, Mabel was Mack's girl friend. After they parted company she led a tumultuous life, becoming the mistress of the director William Desmond Taylor, who was assassinated in mysterious circumstances. Shortly before she died, she married the actor Lew Cody. Undoubtedly Chaplin was not immune to Mabel's charms, but Mack was never far away . . .

Mack Sennett

Mabel Normand

Working with Sennett he learned about comedy, pathos and feeling

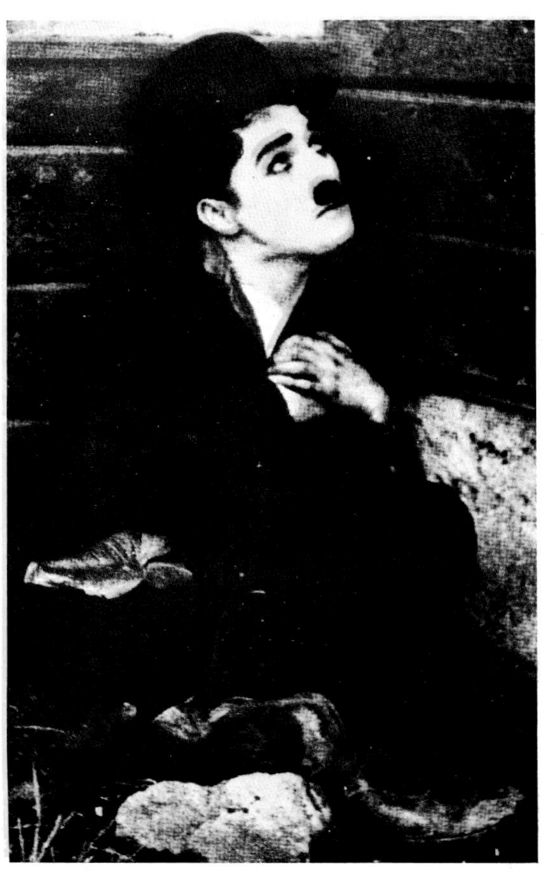

Within the space of less than a year (2 February–7 December 1914), Charles Spencer Chaplin was transformed into Charlie Chaplin, and appeared in thirty-five films

The Keystone films (1914)

Thirty-five films were shot in all, of which twenty-three were directed by Chaplin. With the exception of *Making a Living*, they were all filmed by the same cameraman, Frank D. Williams. Most of Chaplin's shorts have a number of alternative re-release titles; these have been listed in addition to the title in most general use. The date shown in brackets is that of the film's release.

More like Max Linder than Charlie the Tramp, but he already has the walking-stick . . .

1 **Making a Living**
1 reel (2 February 1914)
Alternative titles: A BUSTED JOHNNY. TROUBLES. DOING HIS BEST.
Director: Henry Lehrman. Photography: E.J. Vallejo. Cast: Charles Chaplin, Chester Conklin, Alice Davenport, Minta Durfee, Virginia Kirtley, Henry Lehrman.

A newspaper man passes himself off as a gentleman. He seduces a rich girl and steals her fiancé's job.

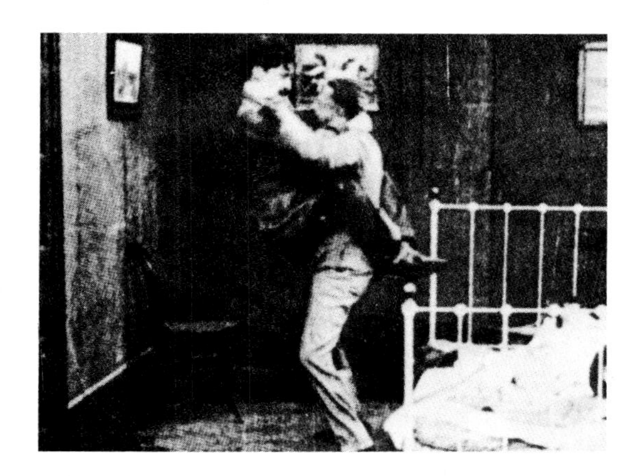

Kid Auto Races at Venice

2 **Kid Auto Races at Venice**
1 reel (7 February 1914)
Director: Henry Lehrman. Photography: Frank Williams. Cast: Charles Chaplin, Charlotte Fitzpatrick, Gordon Griffith, Billy Jacobs, Thelma Salter.

A tramp disrupts the filming of a children's soap-box car race.

Action still with Henry 'Pathé' Lehrman and the cameraman Frank D. Williams

Charlie gets acquainted with the camera

'He borrowed Fatty's trousers, Chester Conklin's old shoes, and got the rest of his clothes from the dressing-room he shared with the other comics and from the studio wardrobe. A few days later we were getting ready to go out to Venice, where there is an amusement park, like Coney Island but on a smaller scale of course, and I saw Chaplin arrive wearing the costume that was to make him famous. His moustache consisted of a rectangle of black crêpe glued under his nose. He seemed delighted with his appearance and twirled his walking-stick with his fingers, a big safety pin took the place of the button missing from his jacket . . .

'And that's how we got to see Charlie Chaplin for the first time in his "trampy" disguise, in the film *Kid Auto Races*, which wasn't supposed to be anything more than a light-hearted documentary about kids, but which became his second film.'

Henry Lehrman

Mabel's Strange Predicament

3 **Mabel's Strange Predicament**
1 reel (9 February 1914)
Alternative title: HOTEL MIX-UP
Directors: Mack Sennett and Henry Lehrman. Cast: Charles Chaplin, Chester Conklin, Alice Davenport, Harry McCoy, Hank Mann, Al St John, Mabel Normand.

The ingredients are Charlie, a small hotel, a call-box, a dog and Mabel's bedroom.

'In *Mabel's Strange Predicament* Chaplin introduced for the first time the business of hopping on one leg as he turned the corner. The famous shuffling walk had already been seen in *Kid Auto Races*, when he broke into a run wearing Chester Conklin's old shoes. In the films after that, whenever he was being chased by a policeman he would bring in the gag of hopping to slow himself down: he would arrive at full tilt at the street corner and, carried forward by his own impetus, in order to stop himself falling or crashing into a passer-by, would screech to a halt on one leg, lifting the other right off the ground. At the same time he would make windmills in the air with his walking-stick, using it to keep his balance, and then, after casting a look behind him to make sure the policeman was still at a safe distance, he was off again, holding his bowler on with his left hand.'

Robert Florey

Between Showers

With Ford Sterling. In the background, Chester Conklin and Emma Clifford

4 **Between Showers**
1 reel (28 February 1914)
Alternative titles: THE FLIRTS. CHARLIE AND THE UMBRELLA. IN WRONG.
Director: Henry Lehrman. Cast: Charles Chaplin, Ford Sterling, Chester Conklin, Emma Clifford, Sadie Lampe.

Charlie and the man with the goatee are rivals for an umbrella and a pretty girl.

5 **A Film Johnnie** ▷
1 reel (2 March 1914)
Alternative titles: MILLION DOLLAR JOB. MOVIE NUT. CHARLIE AT THE STUDIO.
Producer supervising direction: Mack Sennett. Cast: Charles Chaplin, Roscoe 'Fatty' Arbuckle, Virginia Kirtley, Minta Durfee.

Charlie wreaks havoc in a movie studio.

6 **Tango Tangles**
1 reel (9 March 1914)
Alternative titles: CHARLIE'S RECREATION. MUSIC HALL.
Producer supervising direction: Mack Sennett. Cast: Charles Chaplin, Ford Sterling, Roscoe 'Fatty' Arbuckle, Chester Conklin.

Charlie and Fatty go dancing (below). ▽

A famous gag: Charlie lights a cigarette with his revolver

With Fatty

His Favourite Pastime

7 **His Favourite Pastime**
1 reel (16 March 1914)
Alternative titles: THE BONEHEAD. RECKLESS FLING.
Director: George Nichols. Cast: Charles Chaplin, Roscoe 'Fatty' Arbuckle, Peggy Pearce (also known as Viola Barry).

Charlie is caught between the bar, a beauty and her jealous husband.

Cruel, Cruel Love
The Star Boarder

8 **Cruel, Cruel Love**
1 reel (26 March 1914)
Alternative title: LORD HELPUS
Producer supervising direction: Mack Sennett. Cast: Charles Chaplin, Chester Conklin, Alice Davenport, Minta Durfee.

The plot involves a lord, a maid, a fiancée and some poison.

This time he's a lord! And they all think he's poisoned himself for love

9 **The Star Boarder**
1 reel (4 April 1914)
Alternative titles: THE HASH-HOUSE HERO. LANDLADY'S PET.
Producer supervising direction: Mack Sennett. Cast: Charles Chaplin, Alice Davenport, Gordon Griffith, Edgar Kennedy.

Charlie is in love with his landlady.

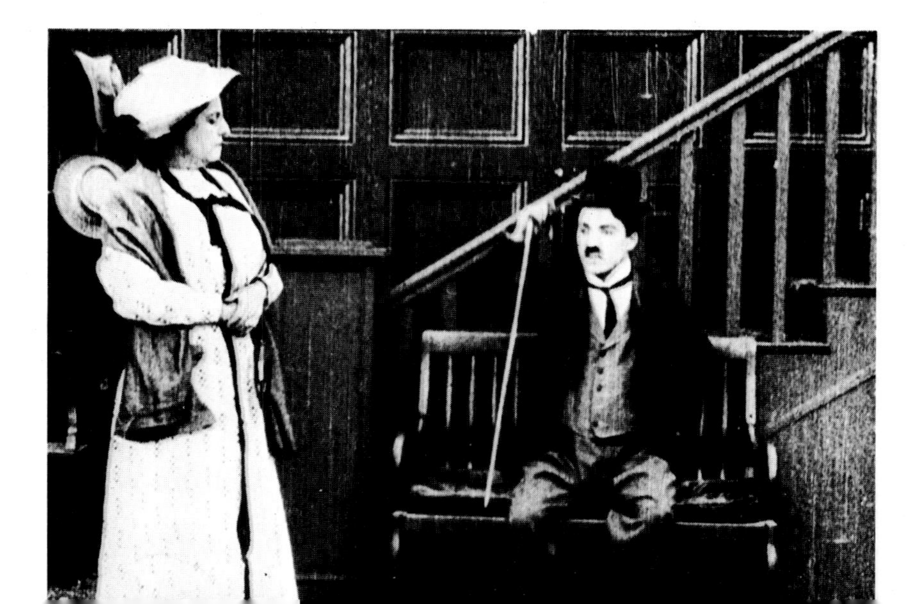

Mabel at the Wheel
Twenty Minutes of Love

Above and below: *Mabel at the Wheel* was Chaplin's first 'two-reeler', directed by Mabel Normand. Charlie wears frock-coat and top hat, and sports an evil-looking tufted goatee. It was shot in a single day!

◁ 10 **Mabel at the Wheel**
2 reels (18 April 1914)
Alternative titles: HIS DAREDEVIL QUEEN. HOT FINISH.
Directors: Mack Sennett and Mabel Normand. Cast: Charles Chaplin, Mabel Normand, Chester Conklin, Harry McCoy, Al St John, Bill Seiter, Mack Sennett.

Charlie and Mabel are racing drivers.

11 **Twenty Minutes of Love**
1 reel (20 April 1914)
Alternative titles: HE LOVED HER SO. COPS AND WATCHES. LOVE FRIEND.
Producer supervising direction: Mack Sennett. Cast: Charles Chaplin, Chester Conklin, Minta Durfee, Gordon Griffith, Edgar Kennedy, Joseph Swickard, Hank Mann.

Spring is in the air, and a watch ends up in someone else's pocket. ▽

12 **Caught in a Cabaret**
2 reels (27 April 1914)
Alternative titles: THE WAITER. JAZZ WAITER. FAKING WITH SOCIETY.
Directors: Mabel Normand and Charles Chaplin. Screenplay: Charles Chaplin. Cast: Charles Chaplin, Mabel Normand, Minta Durfee, Gordon Griffith, Alice Howell, Edgar Kennedy, Harry McCoy, Wallace McDonald, Mack Swain, Alice Davenport, Chester Conklin, Phyllis Allen, Hank Mann, Joseph Swickard, Leo White.

Hi-jinks in the café where Mabel and her fiancé are looking for a crazy clergyman.

Chaplin takes matters into his own hands and decides to direct his films himself. Mack Sennett agrees: 'But Mabel will keep an eye on you.'

Caught in the Rain

13 **Caught in the Rain**
1 reel (4 May 1914)
Alternative titles: AT IT AGAIN. WHO GOT STUNG?
Director/Screenplay: Charles Chaplin. Cast: Charles Chaplin, Alice Davenport, Alice Howell, Mack Swain.

The perils of loving a sleepwalker!

Working on location, Charlie completed the film in a morning

A Busy Day
The Fatal Mallet

◁ 14 **A Busy Day**
Split reel, in tandem with a documentary short called *The Morning Papers* (7 May 1914)
Alternative titles: MILITANT SUFFRAGETTE. LADY CHARLIE.
Director/Screenplay: Charles Chaplin. Cast: Charles Chaplin, Phyllis Allen, Mack Swain.

Charlie is in drag for this tale of a jealous wife.

Penny-pinching again, Chaplin takes over the Alice Davenport part

15 **The Fatal Mallet**
1 reel (1 June 1914)
Alternative titles: THE PILE DRIVER. THE RIVAL SUITORS.
Directors: Charles Chaplin, Mabel Normand and Mack Sennett. Cast: Charles Chaplin, Mabel Normand, Mack Swain, Mack Sennett.

Charlie and Mack Sennett fight to win Mabel's heart – the weapon is a mallet.

Chaplin is partnered by Mack Sennett in this film – the first time we see Charlie kick someone's behind – and it's a lady's! ▽

Her Friend the Bandit
The Knock Out
Mabel's Busy Day

◁ 16 **Her Friend the Bandit**
1 reel (4 June 1914)
Alternative titles: A THIEF CATCHER. MABEL'S FLIRTATION.
Directors: Charles Chaplin and Mabel Normand.
Cast: Charles Chaplin, Charles Murray, Mabel Normand.

A French aristocrat proves to be a bandit in disguise (left).

17 **The Knock Out**
2 reels (11 June 1914)
Alternative titles: COUNTED OUT. THE PUGILIST.
Producer supervising direction: Mack Sennett. Cast: Charles Chaplin, Roscoe 'Fatty' Arbuckle, Charley Chase, Minta Durfee, Alice Howell, Edgar Kennedy, Hank Mann, Al St John, Mack Swain, Mack Sennett, Slim Summerville, Fred Mace, the Keystone Cops.

With Charley as the ref and Fatty as a boxer, chaos ensues (below). ▽

18 **Mabel's Busy Day**
1 reel (13 June 1914)
Alternative titles: HOT DOGS. CHARLIE AND THE SAUSAGES. LOVE AND LUNCH.
Directors: Charles Chaplin and Mabel Normand.
Cast: Charles Chaplin, Billie Bennett, Chester Conklin, Harry McCoy, Wallace MacDonald, Mabel Normand, Slim Summerville, Edgar Kennedy, Al St John, Charley Chase.

At the races. Charlie, Mabel and some hot dogs (below). ▽

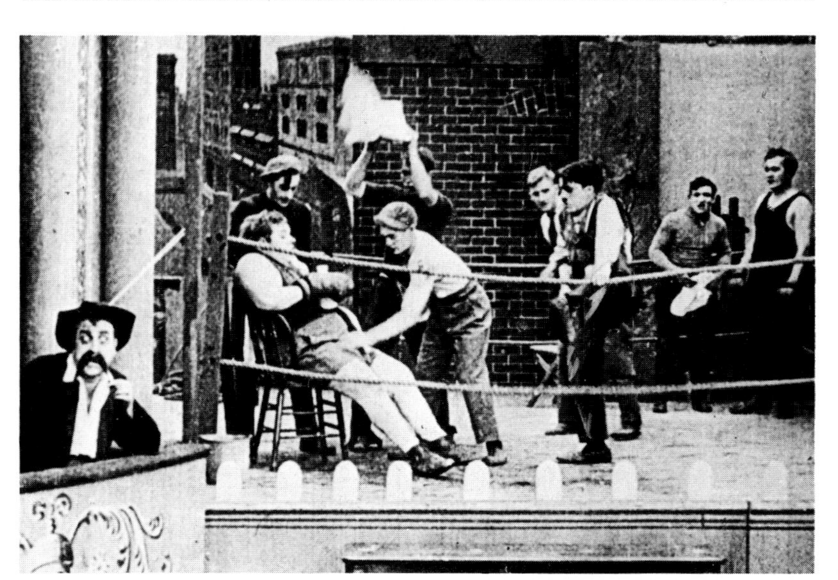

Mabel's Married Life

19 **Mabel's Married Life**
1 reel (20 June 1914)
Alternative titles: THE SQUAREHEAD. WHEN YOU'RE MARRIED.
Directors: Charles Chaplin and Mabel Normand.
Cast: Charles Chaplin, Alice Davenport, Alice Howell, Harry McCoy, Wallace MacDonald, Charles Murray, Mabel Normand, Mack Swain, Hank Mann, Mack Sennett.

The problems of married life.

Alone at last!

The Property Man
Laughing Gas

20 **Laughing Gas**
1 reel (9 July 1914)
Alternative titles: TUNING HIS IVORIES. THE DENTIST. DOWN AND OUT.
Director/Screenplay: Charles Chaplin. Cast: Charles Chaplin, Alice Howell, Fritz Schade, Slim Summerville, Joseph Sutherland, Mack Swain, Joseph Swickard.

The dentist's assistant takes over.

The first film written and directed by Chaplin working entirely on his own

The kick on the behind becomes a running gag, and the mallet makes a comeback

21 **The Property Man**
2 reels (1 August 1914)
Alternative titles: THE ROUSTABOUT. GETTING HIS GOAT. VAMPING VENUS.
Director/Screenplay: Charles Chaplin. Cast: Charles Chaplin, Charles Bennett, Harry McCoy, Lee Morris, Mack Sennett, Phyllis Allen, Mack Swain, Alice Davenport.

Charlie sows confusion in a vaudeville theatre.

A free hand at directing from now on

Recreation
The Masquerader

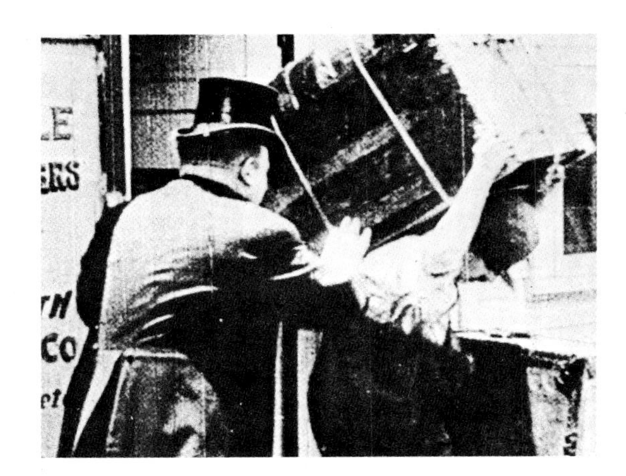

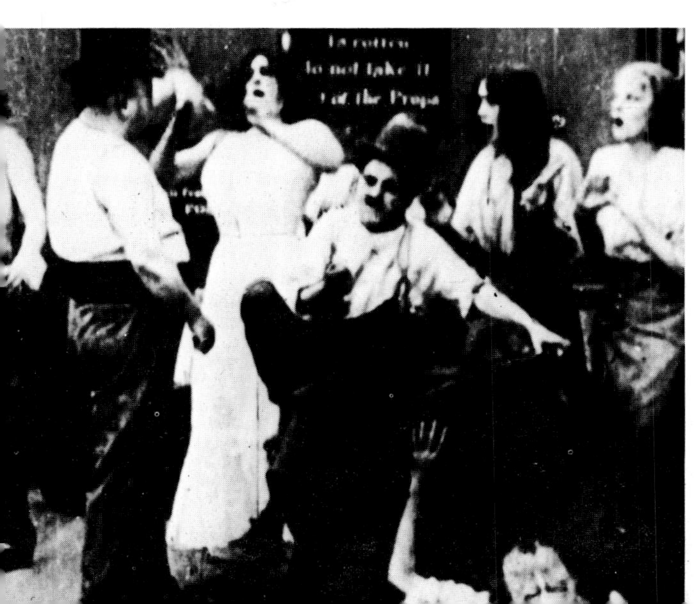

23 **Recreation**
1 reel (13 August 1914)
Alternative title: SPRING FEVER.
Director/Screenplay: Charles Chaplin. Cast: Charles Chaplin, Mabel Normand, Mack Swain, Cecile Arnold, Chester Conklin.

It's the month of May (above), and missiles are flying.

24 **The Masquerader**
1 reel (27 August 1914)
Alternative titles: THE FEMALE IMPERSONATOR. PUTTING ONE OVER. Also, in error: HIS NEW PROFESSION.
Director/Screenplay: Charles Chaplin. Cast: Charles Chaplin, Roscoe 'Fatty' Arbuckle, Cecile Arnold, Charley Chase, Chester Conklin, Minta Durfee, Vivian Edwards, Harry McCoy, Charles Murray, Fritz Schade.

An amorous actor masquerades as a flirtatious female (left and below).

The Masquerader

The Face on the Bar Room Floor

22 **The Face on the Bar Room Floor**
1 reel (10 August 1914)
Alternative titles: THE HAM ARTIST. THE HAM ACTOR.
Director/Screenplay: Charles Chaplin. Based on the poem by Hugh Antoine d'Arcy. Cast: Charles Chaplin, Cecile Arnold, Chester Conklin, Fritz Schade, Vivian Edwards, Minta Durfee, Mack Swain, Hank Mann, Harry McCoy, Wallace MacDonald.

The decline of a great painter whose wife deceives him.

John Ford made a film on the same theme, and with the same title, in 1923.

Painting, boxing and impersonation are three recurrent themes ▷

His New Profession

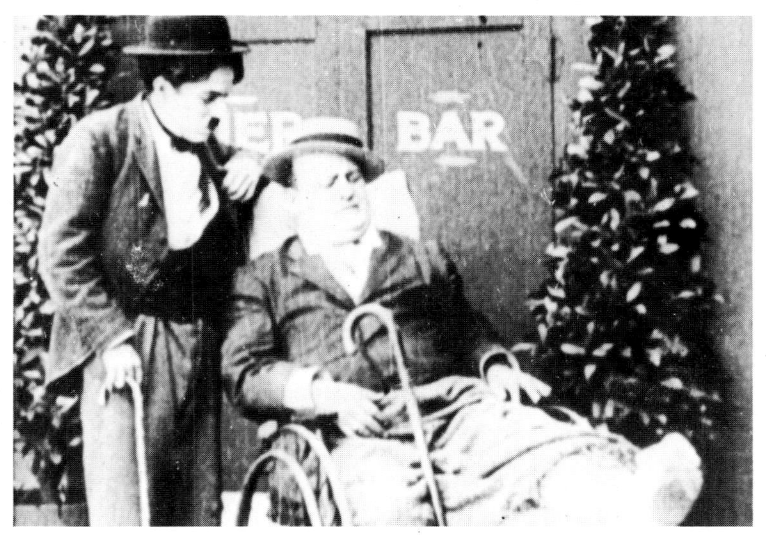

25 **His New Profession**
1 reel (31 August 1914)
Alternative titles: THE GOOD-FOR-NOTHING. HELPING HIMSELF.
Director/Screenplay: Charles Chaplin.. Cast: Charles Chaplin, Charley Chase, Minta Durfee, Harry McCoy, Fritz Schade.

A wheelchair, a blind man who can see, and an unexpected dip in the sea.

The Rounders

26 **The Rounders**
1 reel (7 September 1914)
Alternative titles: OH! WHAT A NIGHT! TWO OF A KIND. REVELRY.
Director/Screenplay. Cast: Charles Chaplin, Roscoe 'Fatty' Arbuckle, Phyllis Allen, Charley Chase, Minta Durfee, Wallace MacDonald, Al St John, Fritz Schade.

Charlie and Fatty escape from their wives for a drunken night out.

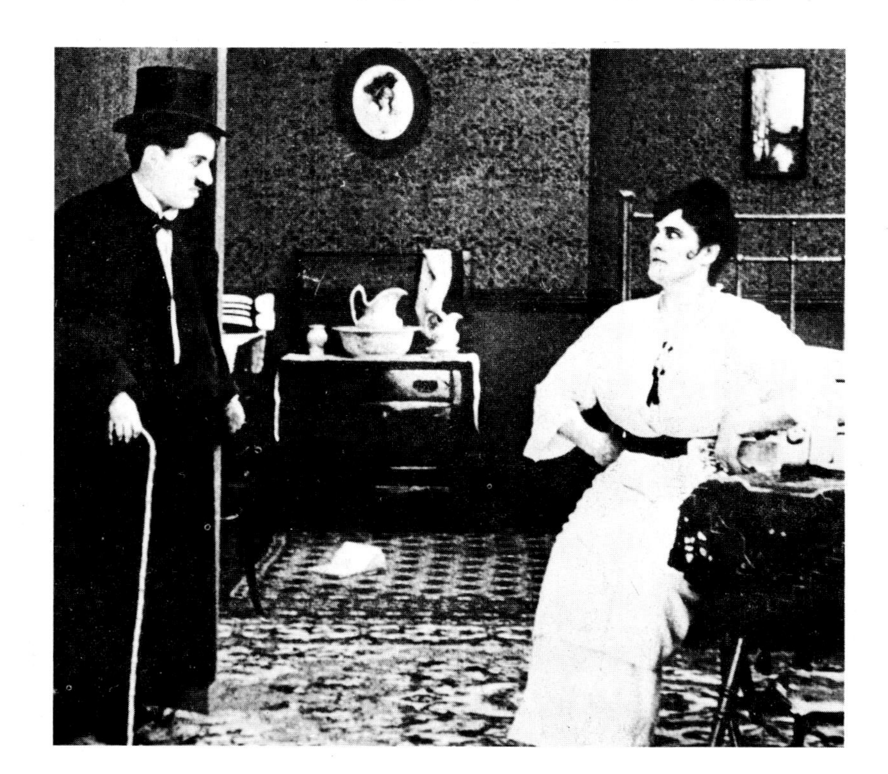

The New Janitor

Charlie's famous gag: taking aim at an intruder with his back still turned – by ducking down and looking through his legs

27 **The New Janitor**
1 reel (24 September 1914)
Alternative titles: THE NEW PORTER. THE BLUNDERING BOOB. THE PORTER.
Director/Screenplay: Charles Chaplin. Cast: Charles Chaplin, Jack Dillon, Minta Durfee, Al St John, Fritz Schade.

The boss gets a soaking, but the thief is caught.

Those Love Pangs

Dough and Dynamite
His Musical Career

◁ 28 **Those Love Pangs**
1 reel (10 October 1914)
Alternative titles: THE RIVAL MASHERS. BUSTED HEARTS.
Director/Screenplay: Charles Chaplin. Cast: Charles Chaplin, Cecile Arnold, Chester Conklin, Vivian Edwards, Edgar Kennedy, Harry McCoy, Norma Nichols.

Fortunately you never really die of love (opposite).

29 **Dough and Dynamite**
2 reels (26 October 1914)
Alternative titles: THE COOK. THE DOUGHNUT DESIGNER.
Director/Screenplay: Charles Chaplin. Based on an idea by Mack Sennett. Cast: Charles Chaplin, Phyllis Allen, Cecile Arnold, Charley Chase, Chester Conklin, Vivian Edwards, Edgar Kennedy, Wallace MacDonald, Norma Nichols, Fritz Schade, Slim Summerville

Pastry dough, custard pies and explosions of mirth! (below). ▽

31 **His Musical Career**
1 reel (7 November 1914)
Alternative titles: THE PIANO MOVERS. MUSICAL TRAMPS.
Direction/Screenplay: Charles Chaplin. Cast: Charles Chaplin, Phyllis Allen, Joe Bordeaux, Charley Chase, Alice Howell, Fritz Schade, Mack Swain.

Pianos that dance by themselves (below). ▽

Gentlemen of Nerve

30 **Gentlemen of Nerve**
1 reel (29 October 1914)
Alternative titles: SOME NERVE. CHARLIE AT THE RACES.
Director/Screenplay: Charles Chaplin. Cast: Charles Chaplin, Phyllis Allen, Charley Chase, Chester Conklin, Alice Davenport, Mabel Normand, Slim Summerville, Mack Swain, Edgar Kennedy.

A penniless flirt contributes to the mayhem at the auto-races.

32 **His Trysting Place** ▷
2 reels (9 November 1914)
Alternative title: FAMILY HOUSE.
Director/Screenplay: Charles Chaplin. Cast: Charles Chaplin, Phyllis Allen, Mabel Normand, Mack Swain.

The problems of married life (continued).

His Trysting Place

Charlie's bowler hat becomes a halo

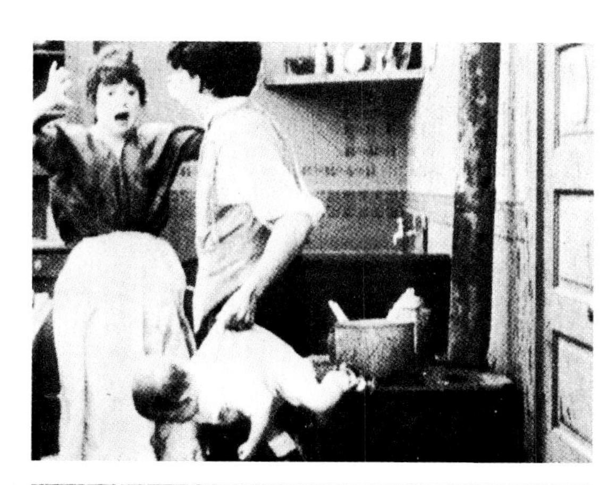

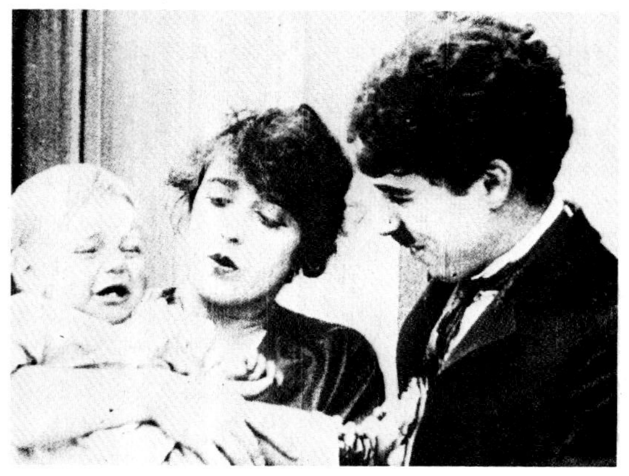

Tillie's Punctured Romance

33 **Tillie's Punctured Romance**
6 reels (14 November 1914)
Alternative titles: TILLIE'S NIGHTMARE. MARIE'S MILLIONS.
Director: Mack Sennett. Screenplay: Hampton Del Ruth. Based on the musical comedy *Tillie's Nightmare* by Edgar Smith. Cast: Charles Chaplin, Marie Dressler, Mabel Normand, Phyllis Allen, Charles Bennett, Charley Chase, Chester Conklin, Minta Durfee, Alice Davenport, Alice Howell, Gordon Griffith, Edgar Kennedy, Harry McCoy, Wallace MacDonald, Charles Murray, Slim Summerville, Hank Mann.
Shot in fourteen weeks (mid-April to August 1914).

Charlie steals the money Tillie has taken from her father, then goes back to Mabel, his accomplice. But Tillie inherits a fortune and Charlie wants marriage. However, the rich uncle turns up alive. A quick-fire succession of gags, chases and rough-and-tumble.

Effectively a feature-length movie. Marie Dressler – who created the stage role in the original operetta – was the star, Chaplin just a member of the cast

Getting Acquainted

34 **Getting Acquainted** △
1 reel (5 December 1914)
Alternative titles: A FAIR EXCHANGE. EXCHANGE IS NO ROBBERY.
Director/Screenplay: Charles Chaplin. Cast: Charles Chaplin, Phyllis Allen, Cecile Arnold, Edgar Kennedy, Harry McCoy, Mabel Normand, Mack Swain.

Let's swap wives! ▽

The last film with Mabel Normand

His Prehistoric Past

35 **His Prehistoric Past**
2 reels (7 December 1914)
Alternative titles: A DREAM. THE CAVEMAN. KING CHARLIE.
Director/Screenplay: Charles Chaplin. Cast: Charles Chaplin, Gene Marsh, Al St John, Fritz Schade, Mack Swain.

Charlie dreams of being a prehistoric herdsman ruling over his harem.

The last film for Mack Sennett

Being free of copyright restrictions, some of the Keystone shorts have occasionally been used in compilation films, of varying quality, in conjunction with films from other sources: THE MACK SENNETT FESTIVAL, WHEN COMEDY WAS KING, etc.

The second phase of Chaplin's career

The Essanay Films (1915)

Fourteen films were made, all directed by Chaplin. Cameraman: Rollie Totheroh. The first film was shot at the Essanay Studios in Chicago, the following five at the Essanay Studio in Niles (near San Francisco), and the remainder at the Bradbury and Majestic Studios in Los Angeles.

Charlie with his mallet, sketch by Cami

1915: The Hollywood straw hat

Hollywood luminaries

1915. 'Charlie Chaplin is the greatest of all the artistes who worked for me . . . If you only knew how much I've regretted losing him . . . Ah! If I could have my time again!' (Mack Sennett in later years). It was Sennett who introduced Chaplin to Thomas Ince and to the famous director D.W. Griffith (above) who had recently discovered the Gish sisters (below)

His New Job

1 **His New Job**
2 reels (1 February 1915)
Alternative title: CHARLIE'S NEW JOB.
Director/Screenplay: Charles Chaplin. Cast: Charles Chaplin, Agnes Ayres, Frank J. Coleman, Charles Insley, Charlotte Mineau, Gloria Swanson, Ben Turpin, Leo White.

Charlie is a studio carpenter but is used as the male lead's double.

The film, Chaplin's Chicago début, was a complete write-off

A Night Out

2 **A Night Out**
2 reels (15 February 1915)
Alternative title: CHAMPAGNE CHARLIE.
Director/Screenplay: Charles Chaplin. Cast: Charles Chaplin, Fred Goodwins, Bud Jamison, Edna Purviance, Ben Turpin, Leo White.

Somewhat the worse for wear, Charlie returns to his hotel with friend Ben Turpin, to be faced with a dog, a pretty woman in her pyjamas, and a jealous husband.

The legendary custard pie

The Champion

3 **The Champion**
2 reels (11 March 1915)
Alternative titles: CHAMPION CHARLIE.
BATTLING CHARLIE.
Director/Screenplay: Charles Chaplin. Cast: Charles Chaplin, Lloyd Bacon, Ben Turpin, Carl Stockdale, Paddy McGuire, Billy Armstrong, Bud Jamison, Edna Purviance, Broncho Billy Anderson.

With his lucky horseshoe inside his glove, Charlie becomes a champion boxer. But he has only his bulldog to help when he's involved in the fight of his life.

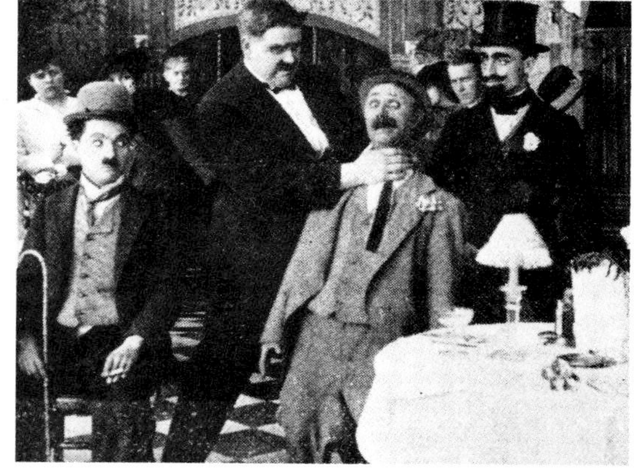

4 **In the Park** △
1 reel (18 March 1915)
Alternative title: CHARLIE ON THE SPREE.
Director/Screenplay: Charles Chaplin. Cast: Charles Chaplin, Lloyd Bacon, Bud Jamison, Edna Purviance, Leo White, Margie Reiger, Billy Armstrong, Ernest van Pelt.

Thieves do respect property – it's just that they want the property to be theirs, so they can respect it all the more! ▽

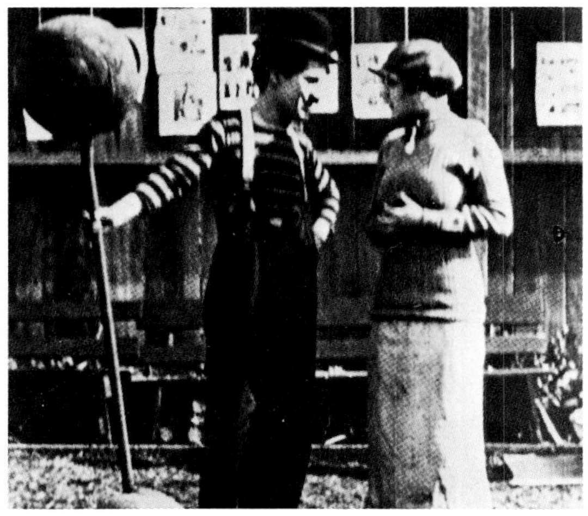

In the Park

A Jitney Elopment

In *The Tramp* the legendary character is fully formed

5 **A Jitney Elopement**
2 reels (1 April 1915)
Alternative titles: MARRIED IN HASTE. CHARLIE'S ELOPEMENT.
Director/Screenplay: Charles Chaplin. Cast: Charles Chaplin, Lloyd Bacon, Fred Goodwins, Paddy McGuire, Edna Purviance, Leo White, Bud Jamison, Carl Stockdale.

Edna is pursued by a horrible Count but Charlie, disguised as an aristocrat, wins her love; along the way there are many alarums and excursions and a final epic chase.

The Tramp

6 **The Tramp**
2 reels (11 April 1915)
Alternative title: CHARLIE THE HOBO.
Director/Screenplay: Charles Chaplin. Cast: Charles Chaplin, Billy Armstrong, Lloyd Bacon, Fred Goodwins, Bud Jamison, Paddy McGuire, Edna Purviance, Leo White, Ernest van Pelt.

The tramp works on a farm. He scares off some ruffians and dreams of marrying the farmer's daughter. But dreams are just dreams . . . the open road is the only life for him.

Back to Los Angeles

7 **By the Sea**
1 reel (29 April 1915)
Alternative title: CHARLIE'S DAY OUT.
Director/Screenplay: Charles Chaplin. Cast: Charles Chaplin, Billy Armstrong, Bud Jamison, Margie Reiger, Edna Purviance, Ben Turpin.

Ice-cream cones, banana skins and a lifebuoy, plus a pretty girl, an angry husband and a cop leading each other a merry dance on the Pacific seashore.

8 **Work**
2 reels (21 June 1915)
Alternative titles: THE PAPER HANGER. THE PLUMBER. CHARLIE AT WORK. ONLY A WORKING MAN.
Director/Screenplay: Charles Chaplin. Cast: Charles Chaplin, Billy Armstrong, Marta Golden, Charles Insley, Paddy McGuire, Edna Purviance, Leo White.

Charlie's a decorator, having problems with ladders, scaffolding, pots of paste and rolls of wallpaper. He loves the maid, but when the mistress's lover appears on the scene it is Charlie who gets blamed by her jealous husband.

By the Sea

A Woman

9 **A Woman**
2 reels (12 July 1915)
Alternative titles: THE PERFECT LADY. CHARLIE AND THE PERFECT LADY.
Director/Screenplay: Charles Chaplin. Cast: Charles Chaplin, Billy Armstrong, Marta Golden, Charles Insley, Edna Purviance, Margie Reiger, Leo White.

In a trick to get rid of his sweetheart's other suitor, Charlie poses as a woman. His rival and his future father-in-law fall head over heels in love with him, until all is revealed!

A Woman

Prophetic images

The real dictator is still some twenty years in the future, and the Great Dictator, twenty-five

10 **The Bank**
2 reels (16 August 1915)
Alternative title: CHARLIE AT THE BANK.
Director/Screenplay: Charles Chaplin. Cast: Charles Chaplin, Billy Armstrong, Lloyd Bacon, Frank Coleman, Fred Goodwins, Charles Insley, Paddy McGuire, Edna Purviance, Wesley Ruggles, John Rand, Carl Stockdale, Carrie Clarke Ward, Leo White.

Just a cleaner at the bank, Charlie juggles with broom, bucket and floorcloth . . . then he outwits the burglars and wins Edna's heart. Sadly, he wakes up among the mops and brushes to find it was just a dream.

Shanghaied

11 **Shanghaied**
2 reels (4 October 1915)
Alternative title: CHARLIE THE SAILOR.
Director/Screenplay: Charles Chaplin. Cast: Charlie Chaplin, Billy Armstrong, Lawrence Bowes, Fred Goodwins, Bud Jamison, Paddy McGuire, Edna Purviance, John Rand, Wesley Ruggles, Leo White.

Charlie is pressed into service as cook's mate on an old tub about to leave port. He doesn't know it's stacked with dynamite and is going to be blown up for the insurance. The stowaway he rescues turns out to be the owner's daughter.

A Night in the Show

12 **A Night in the Show**
2 reels (20 November 1915)
Alternative title: CHARLIE AT THE SHOW.
Director/Screenplay: Charles Chaplin. Cast: Charles Chaplin, Fred Goodwins, Bud Jamison, James Kelly, Dee Lampton, Paddy McGuire Edna Purviance, John Rand, Carrie Clarke Ward, May White.

Charlie is an elegant and tiresome gentleman who pays court to the pretty girl in the seat next to him, managing in the process to tread on everyone's feet and have an argument with a trombone . . . He's also the smart alec in the gallery.

His great love: Edna

Edna Purviance (1894–1958) was discovered by Chaplin when she was a secretary, aged twenty-one, and he gave her her first film part in *A Night Out*. She played the female lead in *Carmen*, and was in all of Chaplin's subsequent movies, until 1923. She and Chaplin were deeply in love.

13 **Carmen**
2 reels (18 December 1915)
(released in a 4-reel version, 22 April 1976)
Director/Screenplay: Charles Chaplin. Cast: Charles Chaplin, Lawrence Bowles, Frank Coleman, Bud Jamison, Jack Henderson, Edna Purviance, John Rand, Wesley Ruggles, Ben Turpin, Leo White, May White.

Charlie loves the cigarette-girl Carmen, fights a duel with Escamillo and stabs his beloved to death. The film is faithful to the plot of the original Bizet opera, except that Carmen is brought back to life, and the toreadors receive many kicks on the behind.

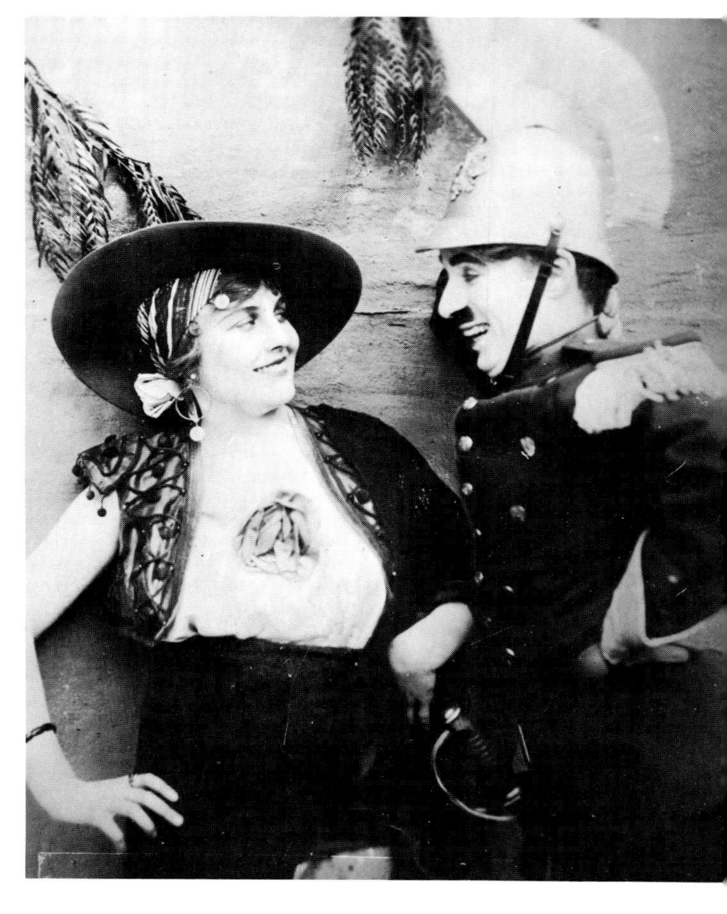

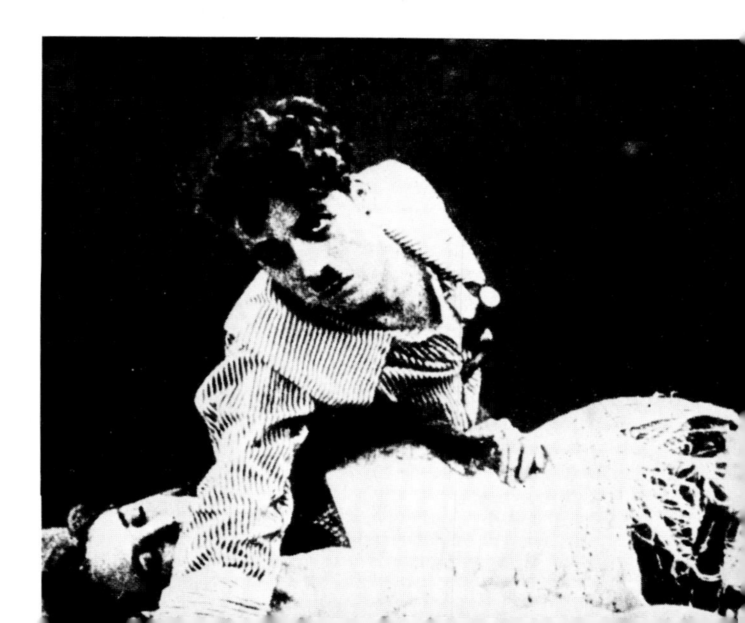

In numerous cinemas all over the USA, Chaplin's *Carmen* (left) was shown as supporting feature to D.W. Griffith's *Intolerance* (above and right)

14 **Police**
2 reels (27 May 1916)
Alternative titles: CHARLIE THE BURGLAR. HOUSEBREAKER
Director/Screenplay: Charles Chaplin. Cast: Charles Chaplin, Billy Armstrong, Frank Coleman, Bud Jamison, Fred Goodwins, James Kelly, Edna Purviance, John Rand, Leo White, Wesley Ruggles.

Just out of prison, Charlie plans a burglary with an ex-prisoner friend. The mistress of the house is pretty and persuasive, but he's soon on the run again with the cops in hot pursuit.

Police

15 Under the title TRIPLE TROUBLE (2 reels, 11 August 1918) Essanay issued a film assembled out of extracts from WORK, POLICE and LIFE (an unfinished Chaplin feature); the actors were Charles Chaplin, Edna Purviance, Leo White, Billy Armstrong, Wesley Ruggles, James Kelly, Bud Jamison and Albert Austin. On 16 September 1916, Essanay had already issued a compilation of 1,500 metres using extracts from other Chaplin films, under the title THE ESSANAY-CHAPLIN REVUE. Other such compilations include: CHASE ME CHARLIE, COMEDY COCKTAIL, CHAPLIN'S ART OF COMEDY, LA GRANDE PARADE DE CHARLOT, etc.

Max Linder: the master

Max Linder (1883–1925) was the greatest French comic of his age, and when Chaplin left Essanay it was to Linder that the company turned for a replacement. Florey was the first to point out that the two men had a strong mutual respect for each other. Max liked to relate that he had been Chaplin's 'professor', and Chaplin did not demur. In fact their styles were quite different, and it would be more accurate to say that Linder gave Chaplin the idea of making films – he would have seen Max Linder in the cinemas of London and Paris well before 1910. The Linder film persona was an elegant Parisian dandy who wore tails and topper, an incorrigible flirt and womanizer.

Above, the ritual kick delivered here by a master of the art – Max Linder in *Le Petit Café*

Left, *Max pratique tous les sports* (1910). Below left, *Max Pedicure* (1914). Below, *Max illusionniste* (1903), directed by Louis Gasnier. Gasnier was one of Max Linder's favourite directors; in those early years of the century he achieved an extraordinary degree of fame as the director of serials like *The Perils of Pauline* and *Mysteries of New York*

The Mutual Films (1916–1917)

Twelve films directed by Chaplin. Photography by Rollie Totheroh and William C. Foster.

The Floorwalker

1 **The Floorwalker**
2 reels (shot in March 1916; released 12 June 1916)
Director/Screenplay: Charles Chaplin. Cast: Charles Chaplin, Albert Austin, Lloyd Bacon, Henry Bergman, Eric Campbell, Frank Coleman, James Kelly, Charlotte Mineau, Edna Purviance, Leo White.

Taking refuge from the cops in a big store, Charlie runs up against the manager and his accomplice, the floorwalker, who plan to steal the takings. The floorwalker is the spitting image of Charlie . . . The escalator provides scope for endless comic routines.

Below, with Lloyd Bacon, the actor, who later turned to directing (*The Singing Fool*, *42nd Street*, *Gold Diggers of 1937*, *The Oklahoma Kid*)

The Floorwalker

The Fireman

2 **The Fireman**
2 reels (shot in May 1916 and released 12 June 1916)
Director/Screenplay: Charles Chaplin. Cast: Charles Chaplin, Albert Austin, Lloyd Bacon, Eric Campbell, Frank Coleman, James Kelly, Edna Purviance, John Rand, Leo White, Henry Bergman.

Charlie is pretty useless as a fireman and is in big trouble, but he rescues a lovely girl from a burning house and ends up a hero.

The Fireman

'To appreciate the full significance of his work, one has to go back in time to the period when it was created. That is true of all major contributions to the history of the cinema. Time muffles their power to shock and diminishes their originality. They are so often borrowed and imitated that they eventually become clichés. What is more, the images lose their freshness, or appear to do so, because they remain exactly the same while their audiences change . . .'

René Clair

The Vagabond

The melting strains of a violin

3 **The Vagabond**
2 reels (shot in June 1916 and released 10 July 1916)
Director/Screenplay: Charles Chaplin. Cast: Charles Chaplin, Albert Austin, Lloyd Bacon, Eric Campbell, Frank Coleman, James Kelly, Charlotte Mineau, Edna Purviance, John Rand, Leo White, Henry Bergman.

Sacked from his job as a violinist in a restaurant, Charlie takes to the road. He plays to a gypsy girl, who turns out to be an heiress abducted as a child. She abandons her handsome painter to go with Charlie to the ends of the earth.

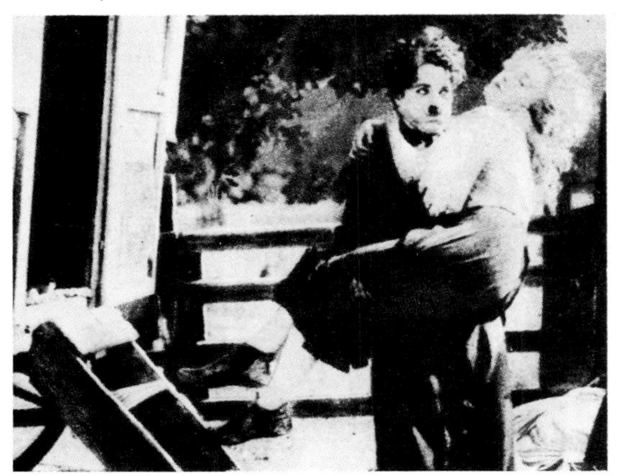

4 **One A.M.**
2 reels (7 August 1916)
Director/Screenplay: Charles Chaplin. Cast: Charles Chaplin, Albert Austin.

A solo performance by Chaplin. Having problems with a staircase, a key, a rug, a carafe, a folding bed and a bathtub.

The theme of a man entangling with recalcitrant objects crops up again and again in Chaplin's films. The *tour de force* is the amazing solo performance he gives in *One A.M.*

One A.M.

The Count

5 **The Count**
2 reels (4 September 1916)
Director/Screenplay: Charles Chaplin. Cast: Charles Chaplin, Albert Austin, Eric Campbell, Frank Coleman, James Kelly, Charlotte Mineau, Edna Purviance, John Rand, Leo White, Leota Bryan, Henry Bergman, Eva Thatcher.

A tailor disguised as a count, Charlie is pursued by his fat boss and flirts with the charming Edna. They tango and waltz – but the real count arrives. Or is he?

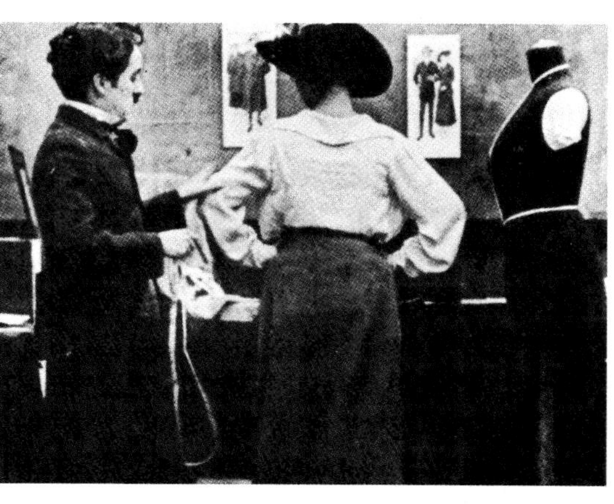

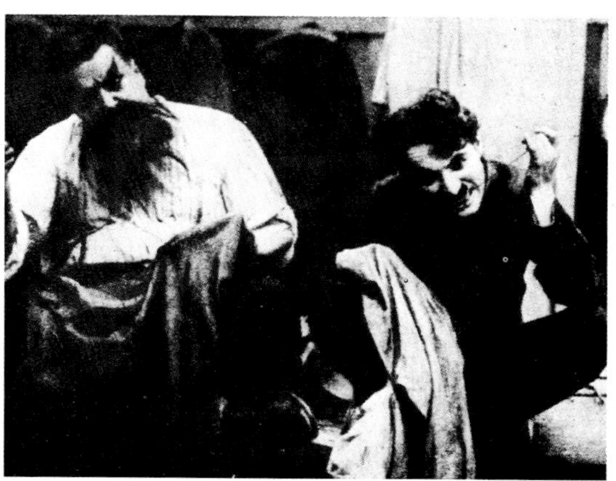

The Count

'Charlie was looking for the right foil and couldn't find him, he didn't want anyone as fat as Arbuckle or as gentle as Swain, but someone taller, much taller than he was, and most difficult of all, a good actor. He'd recently met Eric Campbell, who had some of the qualities he wanted but, big, lovable, fat, clean-shaven fellow that he was, he didn't look in the least bit threatening. So Charlie sent his new villain along to make up and came up with those mephistophelian eyebrows, the wild bushy beard and the big drooping moustache. He turned poor Campbell into a repulsive ogre, a real scarecrow . . .'

Alfred Reeves

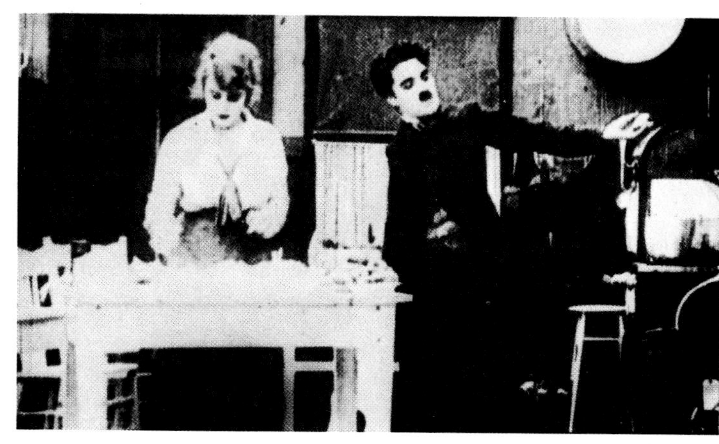

The pawnbroker's assistant

The Pawnshop

6 **The Pawnshop**
2 reels (2 October 1916)
Director/Scriptwriter: Charles Chaplin. Cast: Charles Chaplin, Albert Austin, Henry Bergman, Eric Campbell, Frank Coleman, James Kelly, Edna Purviance, John Rand, Wesley Ruggles.

Charlie works for a pawnbroker and is in love with his boss's daughter. His pal Johnny gets on his nerves and he's ruthless with the customers – a weird procession of people. As for the objects in the shop, they seem to have a will of their own . . .

The Pawnshop

'Neither a borrower nor a lender be . . .'

William Shakespeare

Behind the Screen

7 **Behind the Screen**
2 reels (13 November 1916)
Director/Screenplay: Charles Chaplin. Cast: Charles Chaplin, Albert Austin, Lloyd Bacon, Henry Bergman, Eric Campbell, Frank Coleman, James Kelly, Charlotte Mineau, Edna Purviance, John Rand, Leo White, Leota Bryan, Tom Wood, Wesley Ruggles.

The head carpenter at the film studios has a down on Charlie and overloads him with work. Charlie meets an attractive blonde who wants to break into movies, but it's he who gets a part. In the resulting mayhem the studio is blown up.

Behind the Screen

The Rink

8 **The Rink**
2 reels (4 December 1916)
Director/Screenplay: Charles Chaplin. Cast: Charles Chaplin, Albert Austin, Eric Campbell, Lloyd Bacon, Henry Bergman, Frank Coleman, James Kelly, Charlotte Mineau, Edna Purviance, John Rand.

This time Charlie's a waiter who goes roller-skating. At the rink he rescues Edna from an unwelcome suitor, and demonstrates his acrobatic skills in helter-skelter chases.

The Rink

Easy Street

9 **Easy Street**
2 reels (22 January 1917)
Director/Screenplay: Charles Chaplin. Cast: Charles Chaplin, Albert Austin, Eric Campbell, James Kelly, Frank Coleman, Charlotte Mineau, Edna Purviance, John Rand, Leo White, Janet Miller Sully, Loyal Underwood, Henry Bergman, Lloyd Bacon.

The tramp has become a policeman and boldly confronts the local villain. It's David and Goliath – Charlie bends the lamp post and traps the tough guy's head inside, then turns on the gas. The mean streets are safe to walk again.

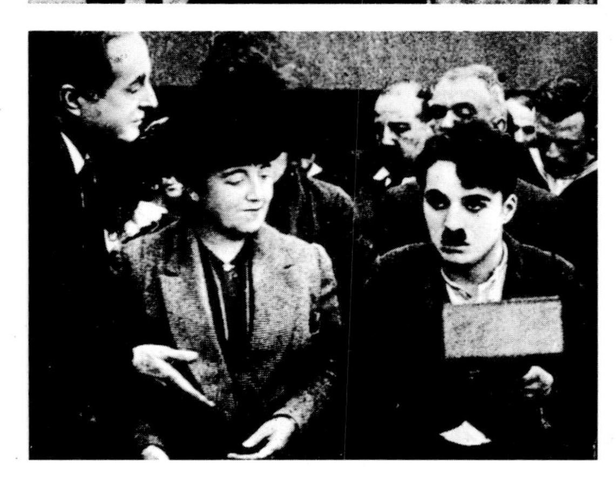

Easy Street

Easy Street

Left, the gag of the tough guy trapped in the lamp

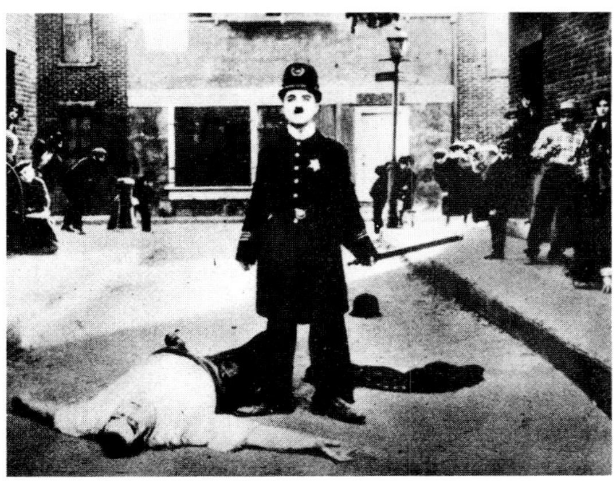

The Cure

10 **The Cure**
2 reels (16 April 1917)
Director/Screenplay: Charles Chaplin. Cast: Charles Chaplin, Albert Austin, Henry Bergman, Eric Campbell, Frank Coleman, James Kelly, Edna Purviance, John Rand, Janet Miller Sully, Loyal Underwood, Tom Wood, Leota Bryan.

Charlie goes to a spa to take the waters – but drinks quantities of whisky too. He escapes from a pummelling by a sadistic masseur only to discover that his bottles of drink have been poured into the spa pool, to the vast delight of the other visitors!

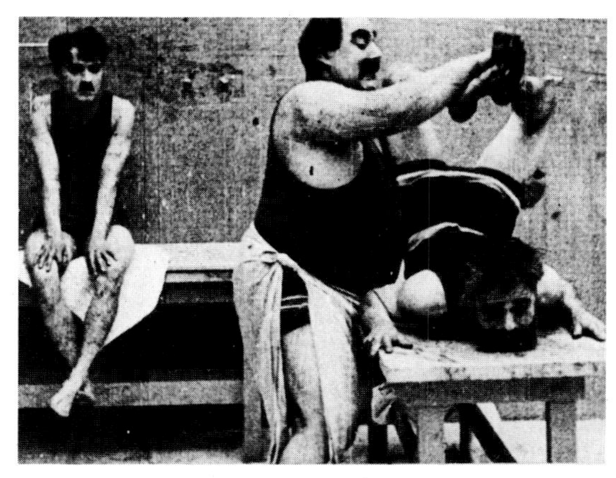

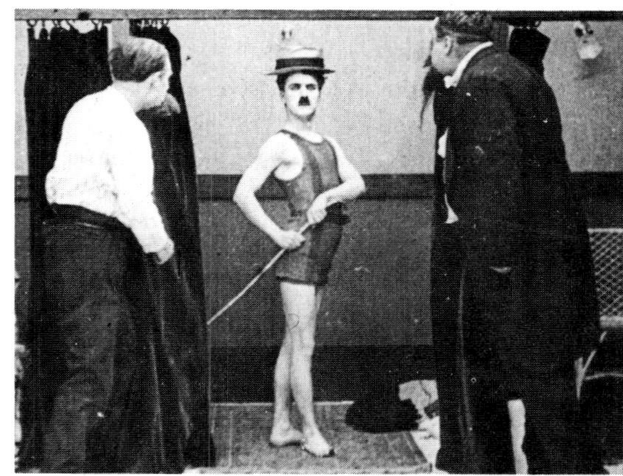

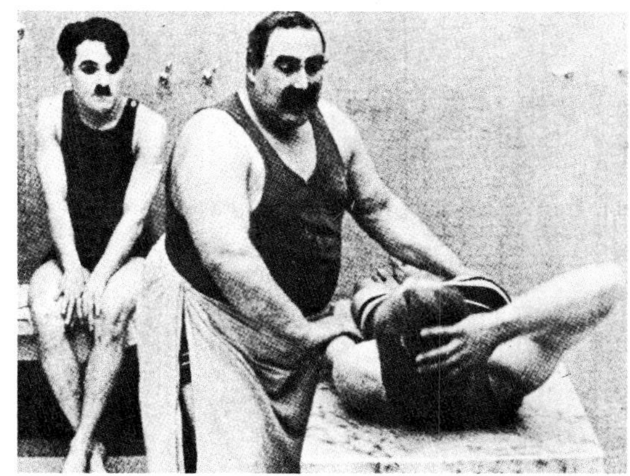

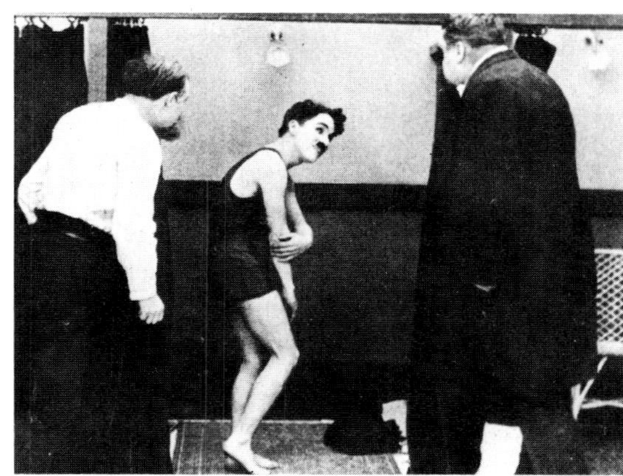

The Cure

The Immigrant

Vivid memories of a real immigrant . . .

11 **The Immigrant**
2 reels (17 June 1917)
Alternative title: THE REFUGEE.
Director/Screenplay: Charles Chaplin. Cast: Charles Chaplin, Albert Austin, Henry Bergman, Eric Campbell, Frank Coleman, James Kelly, Edna Purviance, John Rand, Stanley Sanford, Loyal Underwood, Kitty Bradbury.

Steaming towards the Statue of Liberty is an old tub full of immigrants. On board are Charlie, a Russian Jew, a con-man and Edna. The immigration authorities treat them like cattle. Months later Charlie the Tramp finds five dollars, meets Edna by chance and invites her to dinner. Alas, there's a hole in his pocket and he can't pay the bill – until he spies a tip left conveniently on a plate.

The Immigrant

'He is the brother of Pierrot, rival to Harlequin. With the body of Punchinello, the heart of Cherubino, a man of wit. Like the classic characters he is becoming a myth, entering a world of fairytale, an embellishment to childish pleasures and dreams . . . Our age will pass, the cinema may die, but Chaplin will live on . . .'

Harry Baur (1920)

The Adventurer

12 **The Adventurer**
2 reels (shot in July 1917, and released 23 October 1917)
Director/Screenplay: Charles Chaplin. Cast: Charles Chaplin, Albert Austin, Monta Bell, Henry Bergman, Eric Campbell, Frank Coleman, Toraichi Kono, Edna Purviance, Janet Miller Sully, Loyal Underwood, Marta Golden, James Kelly, John Rand, May White, Phyllis Allen.

Charlie is an escaped convict who saves a rich girl and her mother from drowning. As a guest at the family mansion he leads a life of luxury, until his photograph is published in the newspaper.

A number of compilations with Essanay films have been released: *The Chaplin Festival* (1943), *The Funniest Man in the World* (1967), etc.

The Adventurer

1920. Already fêted as the great Chaplin

Hollywood, cinema capital of the world

1890. Landscape (the future site of Hollywood) . . .

and Hollywood landscape, with figure

The dream factory, otherwise Chaplin's studio – with guard

An old dog kept guard at the entrance used by the studio cars. When Chaplin arrived, the watchdog would prick up its ears and give a feeble wag of its tail, waiting for a pat. Chaplin was deeply distressed when it died. A new dog appeared the very next day.

A turning-point

. . . a woman (Mildred Harris)

Honeymoon trophy

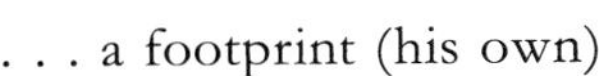

. . . a footprint (his own)

In the early summer of 1917, Chaplin accepted the First National Company's offer of a million dollars to make eight films.

This was when he decided to build his own studio, where he could work without interference.

When it was completed, he put on the Tramp's famous big shoes and marked his footprints in the wet cement. With the tip of his cane he traced his name and the date: 21 January 1918.

This idea was later exploited by the owner of the nearby Grauman Chinese Theatre, who made a collection of the foot- and handprints of Hollywood's big stars.

On 23 October of the same year, Chaplin married the girl-actress Mildred Harris (1901-44). They were divorced in 1920.

The First National Films (1918–1922)

Eight feature-length films and one short were shot between January 1918 and October 1922 in Chaplin's Hollywood studios. As producer, Chaplin held the copyright on his own films. Photography by Rollie Totheroh.

1 **A Dog's Life**
860m (shot in January/March 1918, and released 14 April 1918)
Director/Screenplay: Charles Chaplin. Cast: Charles Chaplin, Albert Austin, Henry Bergman, Sydney Chaplin, Bud Jamison, Park Jones, James Kelly, Edna Purviance, Chuck Riesner, Janet Miller Sully, Loyal Underwood, Billy White, Tom Wilson.

Charlie is out of a job, his only friend a starving mongrel. They work as a team to steal bits of food and end up at the Green Lantern café, where Charlie sees Edna and is smitten. The dog finds a wallet stolen by two scoundrels, the crooks get it back, there's a general scrimmage with Charlie emerging the victor. He takes up farming, marries Edna – and the dog fathers many puppies.

A Dog's Life

A Dog's Life

Chaplin knew that it is always the little man who gets the sympathy of the crowd. He described how he deliberately accentuated his vulnerability by hunching his shoulders, pulling a sorrowful face, adopting a frightened air. If he had been taller, he once said, he would have found it harder to be sympathetic.

'His "sense of humour" was quite different from ours, he analyzed situations and gave them a human dimension, he supplied a motivation for the kicks on the behind and the tumbles, giving them a reason for being there, he "toned down" our burlesque by injecting his own "touches". He was inventive, he explained patiently the whys and wherefores of the things he asked us to do. He took situations that would in ordinary circumstances have appeared tragic, and used them to be funny. His work was clear and simple. It had class. He was always inspired by a spirit of comic imitation, and brought a dancer's grace to all his gestures, juggling with the props and inventing "gags" that only he could put across. While we were satisfied if we caught or threw our missiles fast enough and in the right order, for him chucking a brickbat was a sort of ballet.'

Alfred St John

A Dog's Life

The war is far away . . .

The First World War inspired films like Abel Gance's unforgettable *J'accuse*. It also gave rise to burlesques such as Mack Sennett's *Yankee Doodle in Berlin* (1916).

Shoulder Arms

2 **Shoulder Arms**
1,005m (shot during the summer of 1918, and released 20 October 1918)
Director/Screenplay: Charles Chaplin. Cast: Charles Chaplin, Albert Austin, Henry Bergman, Park Jones, Sydney Chaplin, Edna Purviance, Loyal Underwood, Jack Wilson, Tom Wilson, John Rand.

An American camp during the First World War. Charlie does drill, then falls asleep and dreams he's in the trenches, facing shells and mud. Camouflaged as a tree, he outwits the German soldiers, then performs daring deeds to rescue a pretty girl and take the German High Command captive. He has just driven them back to his own side of the lines, when he wakes up.

Shoulder Arms

Charlie discovers the reality of war

Camouflage

. . . and the ultimate in camouflage!

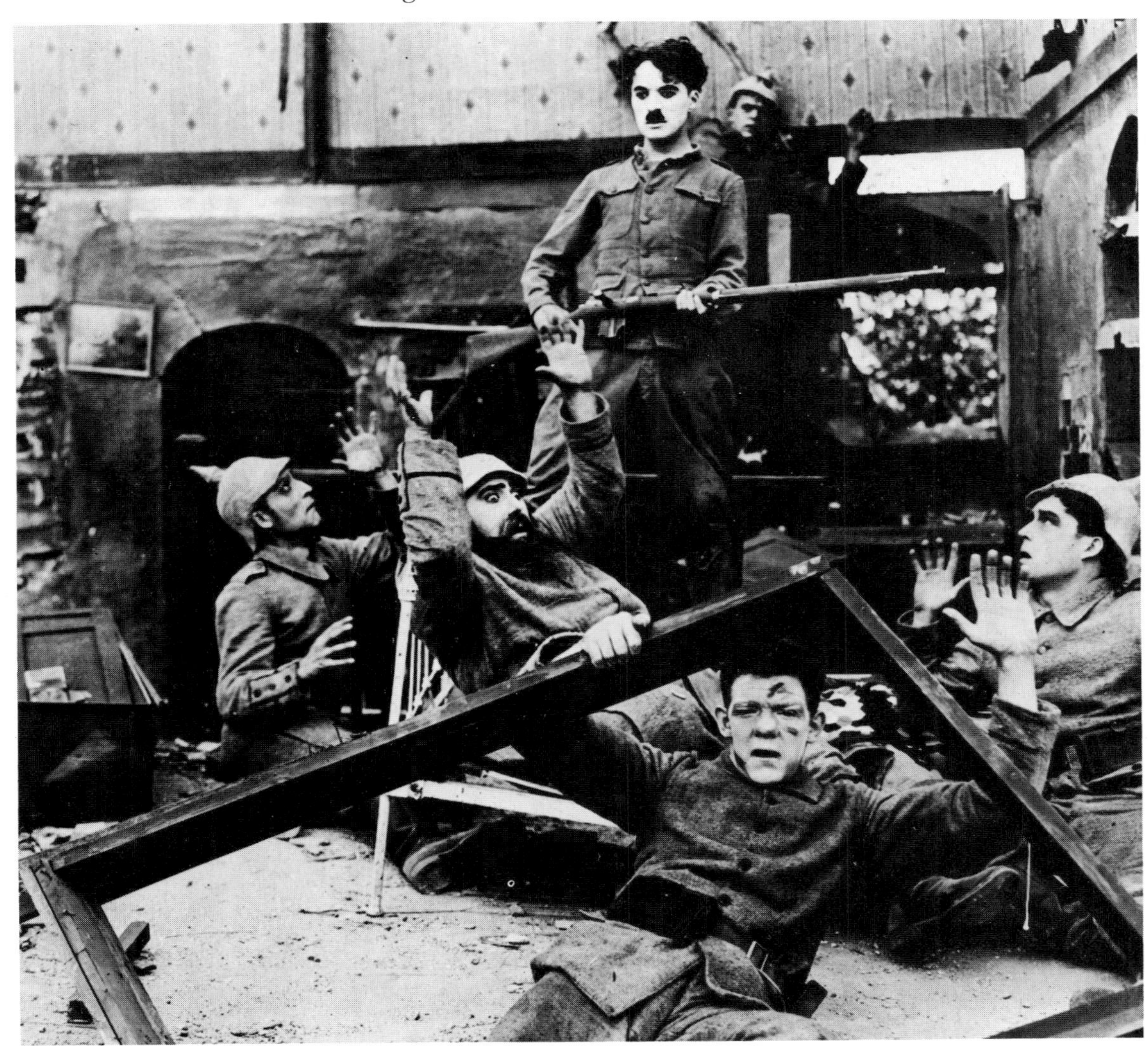

Shoulder Arms

With Edna Purviance as the French girl

With Sydney Chaplin, who played a number of parts including that of Kaiser Wilhelm.

They may look like Hitler and Stalin, but they are not meant to be either

Shoulder Arms

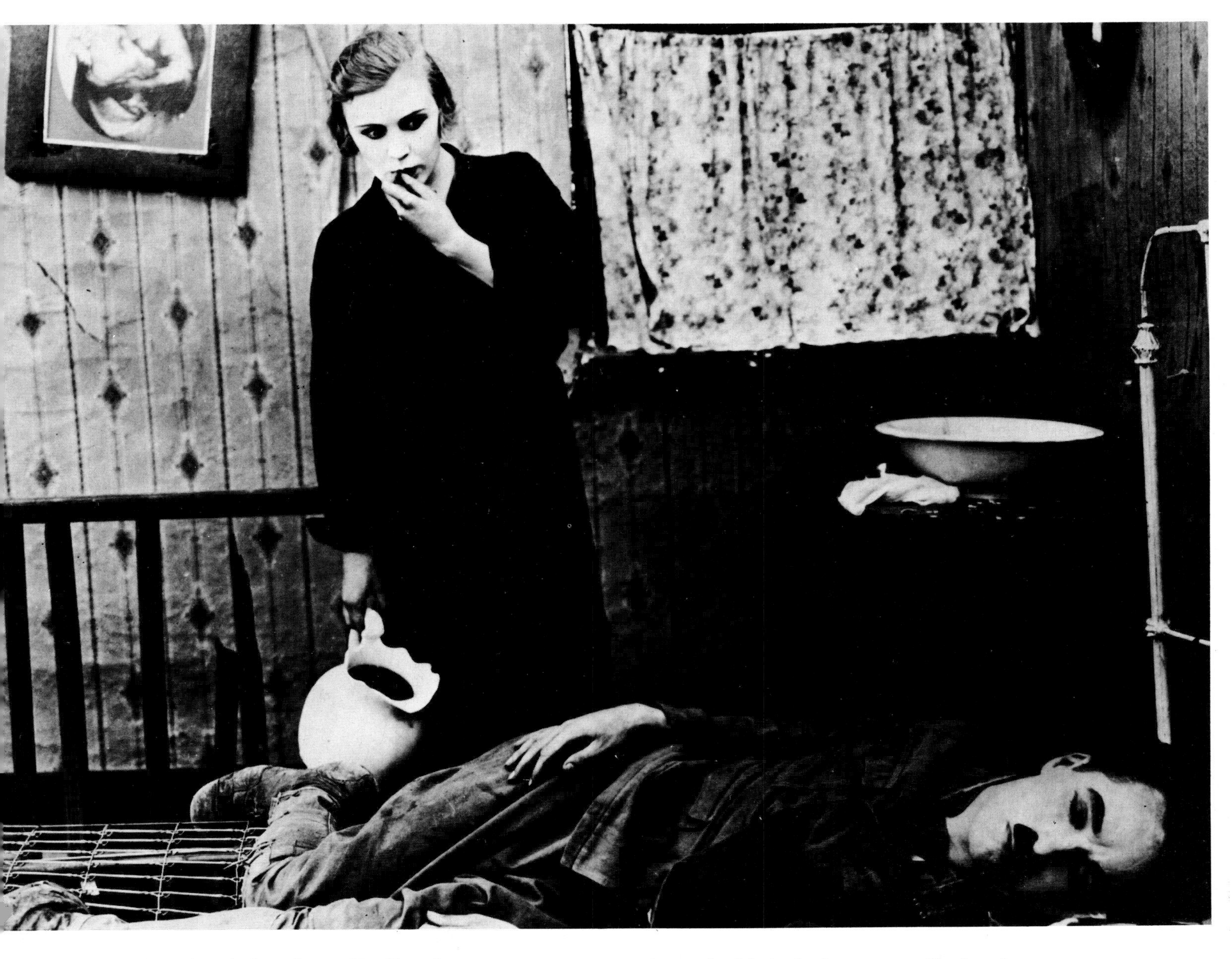

The scene below from *Shoulder Arms* appears in one of the four reels that Chaplin suppressed, although they were edited and complete

The Bond

3 **The Bond**
175m (16 December 1918; special release)
Propaganda film for the Liberty Loan Committee. Director/Screenplay: Charles Chaplin. Cast: Charles Chaplin, Sydney Chaplin, Albert Austin, Edna Purviance.

Three sketches on the themes of love, marriage and liberty. Charlie KOs the Kaiser with his mallet and asks the audience to buy Liberty Bonds.

Opposite, the closing shot of *The Bond*: armed with a mallet (which represents Liberty Bonds), Charlie KOs the Kaiser (Sydney Chaplin)

Chaplin at the ripe old age of thirty . . .

Sunnyside

4 **Sunnyside**
800m (15 June 1919)
Director/Screenplay: Charles Chaplin. Cast: Charles Chaplin, Albert Austin, Henry Bergman, Park Jones, Edna Purviance, Loyal Underwood, Tom Wilson, Tom Terriss, Tom Wood.

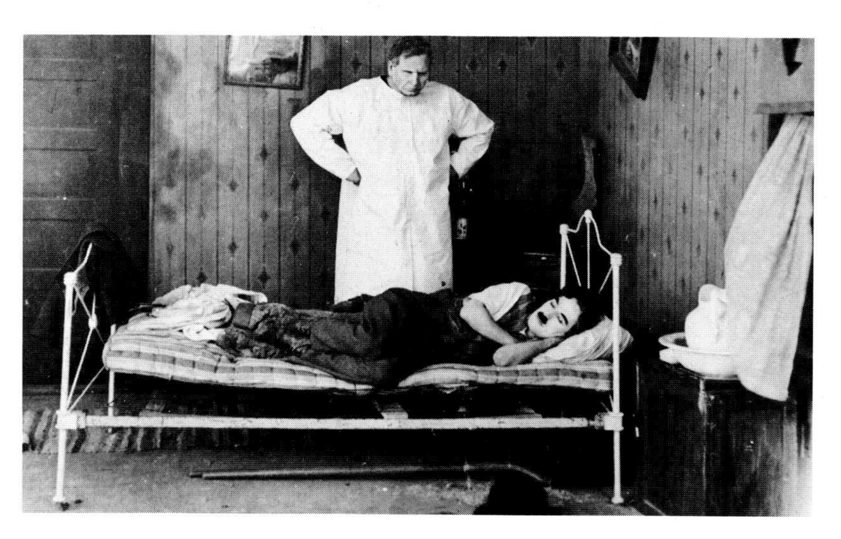

Odd-job man at Sunnyside Farm Hotel, Charlie is browbeaten by his dreadful boss. He loses consciousness after a small argument with some cows, and dreams he is dancing with four nymphs in filmy dresses. To win Edna, who is pursued by another, he throws himself in front of a car . . . and then consciousness returns.

Sunnyside

Sunnyside

Inhabitants of a dream, an idyll

Sunnyside

It is not by chance that I mention the name of Shakespeare. I experience the same sense of sublimity – for instance in *Sunnyside* – the same sense of prodigious artistry, of melancholy depths and fantasy combined.

Elie Faure

A Day's Pleasure

5 **A Day's Pleasure**
550m (7 December 1919)
Director/Screenplay: Charles Chaplin. Cast: Charles Chaplin, Albert Austin, Henry Bergman, Jackie Coogan, Raymond Lee, Babe London, Edna Purviance, Loyal Underwood, Tom Wilson, Mack Swain.

Charlie, his wife and their two boys decide on a quiet day at the seaside. Their old car is on its last legs and gives them heart attacks, the cops turn nasty . . . The family takes a boat trip, Charlie feels ill and rows with the other passengers, and fights a losing battle with a deck-chair.

A Day's Pleasure

The Kid

6 **The Kid**
1,610m (shot 1919–20, and released 17 January 1921)
Director/Screenplay: Charles Chaplin. Cast: Charles Chaplin, Jackie Coogan, Carl Miller, Edna Purviance, Chuck Riesner, Tom Wilson, Albert Austin, Nellie Bly Baker, Monta Bell, Henry Bergman, Lita Grey, Raymond Lee, Phyllis Allen, Sydney Chaplin.

Charlie rescues and brings up an abandoned child. Five years later the kid is breaking windows so Charlie can earn a crust by replacing them! But the mother takes back her child. Charlie wanders the streets in misery until he falls asleep in a doorway – to dream of heaven. He wakes to a better life, where he is reunited with grateful mother and child.

Work is still a game

The Kid

The Kid

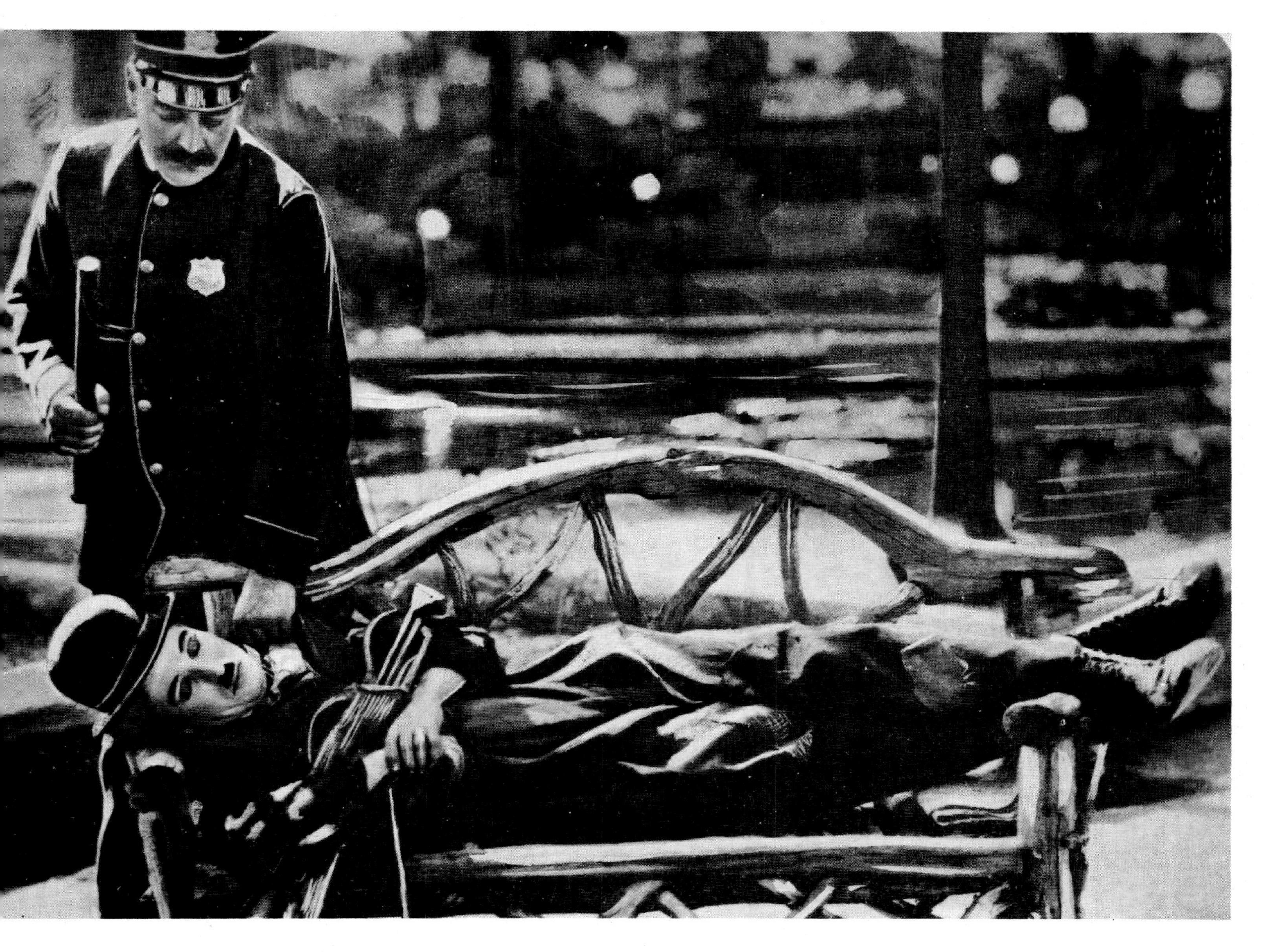

The Idle Class

7 **The Idle Class**
615m (shot in May 1921, and released 25 September 1921)
Director/Screenplay: Charles Chaplin. Cast: Charles Chaplin, Henry Bergman, Allan Garcia, Lita Grey, Lillian McMurray, Edna Purviance, John Rand, Rex Storey, Mack Swain, Loyal Underwood.

Charlie plays both gentleman and tramp. It's the old story of mistaken identity, with the cops and half of high society out to get Charlie.

The Idle Class

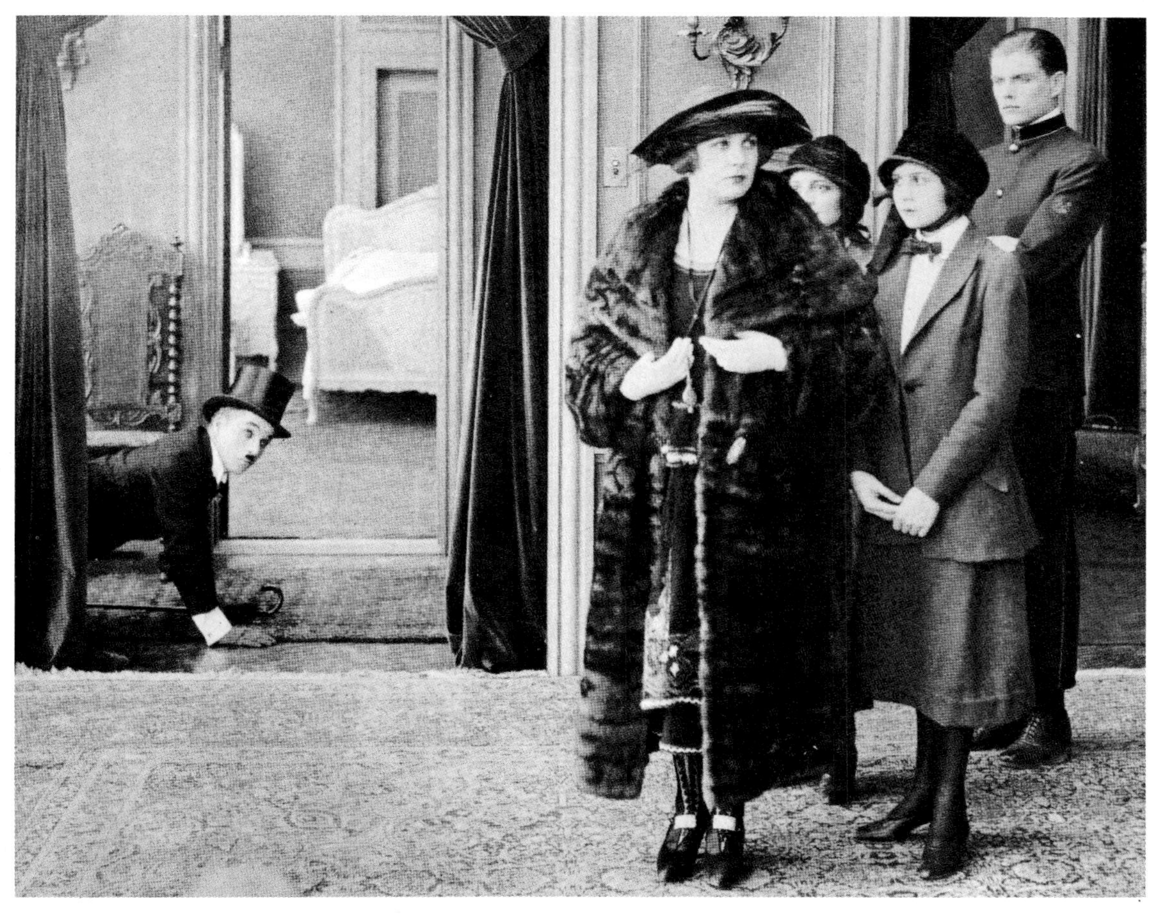

The Idle Class

Pay Day

8 **Pay Day**
610m (shot during the autumn of 1921, and released 15 February 1922)
Director/Screenplay: Charles Chaplin. Cast: Charles Chaplin, Phyllis Allen, Henry Bergman, Allan Garcia, Sydney Chaplin, Edna Purviance, John Rand, Mack Swain, Albert Austin, Loyal Underwood.

Charlie works on a building site and flirts with the foreman's daughter. It's pay day and Charlie's off for a night out with his pals. Of course he misses the last tram and reels home, yet again, to face his irate wife and her rolling pin.

Pay Day

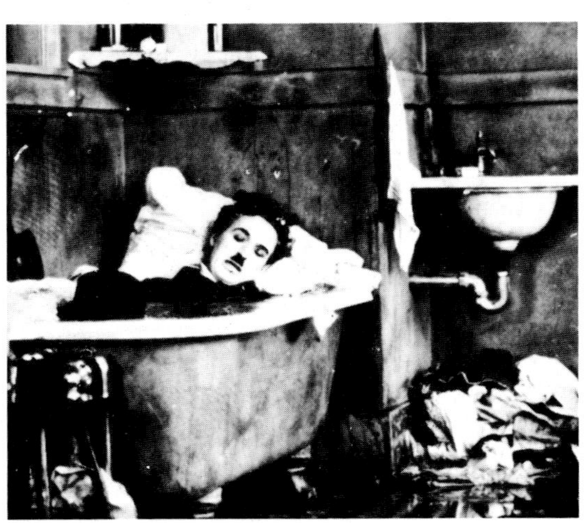

The Pilgrim

9 **The Pilgrim**
1,300m (shot in the summer of 1922, and released 25 February 1923)
Director/Screenplay: Charles Chaplin. Cast: Charles Chaplin, Edna Purviance, Mack Swain, Kitty Bradbury, Dinky Dean, Loyal Underwood, Mai Wells, Sydney Chaplin, Chuck Riesner, Tom Murray, Monta Bell, Edith Bostwick, Henry Bergman, Raymond Lee, Florence Latimer, Phyllis Allen.

A convict on the run, Charlie dresses as a clergyman and finds himself with a church in a Wild West town. He gives a sermon that is a mime of David and Goliath, and is having fun – especially as Edna is his landlady. Then an old cellmate steals Edna's mother's savings. Charlie gets the cash back but is unmasked and run out of town. The Mexican border becomes a tightrope.

First National compilation: THE CHAPLIN REVUE; made by Chaplin, with an added soundtrack, in 1959.

The Pilgrim

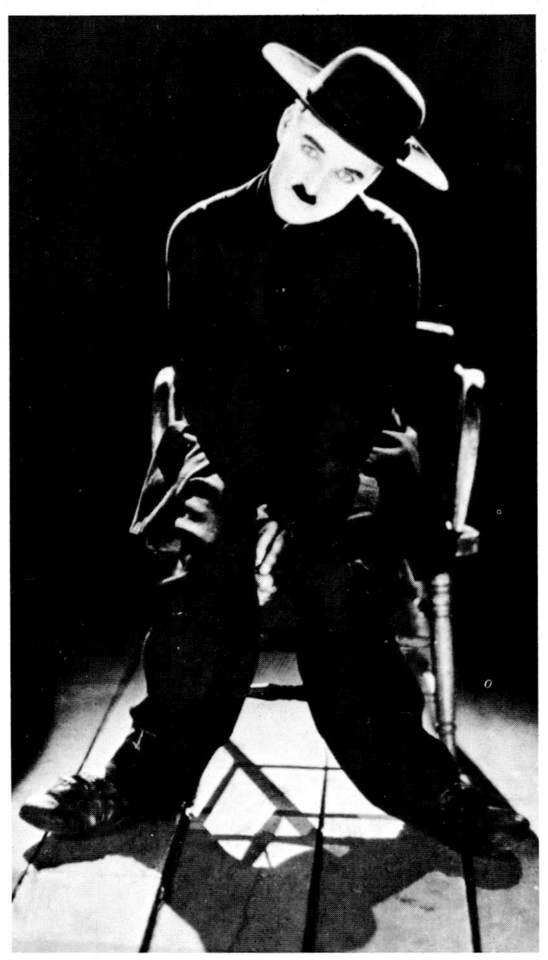

The Pilgrim

The Pilgrim

'An eternal pilgrim on life's hard road, Charlie is greater than his adventures, greater than his personality and his genius; he is humanity itself. That is why each of us understands him in our own way, and why we are in turn intrigued by the depth of our emotion and saddened by our laughter.'

Marcel Brion

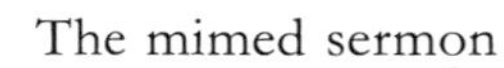

The mimed sermon

The Pilgrim

The great enterprise: United Artists

In 1919 Chaplin had taken the decision, together with his friends D.W. Griffith, Douglas Fairbanks and Mary Pickford, to found a new production company, United Artists.

Because he was still bound by his contract with First National, it was not until 1922 that he made his first independent film.

This association of four of the Hollywood 'giants' marked the real beginnings of the American film industry. For Chaplin it meant a farewell to short and medium-length films and the start of a new phase of his career: in all, he went on to produce nine feature-length movies for United Artists, eight of which were released.

The United Artists Corporation (1923–1952)

Eight feature-length films were directed by Charles Chaplin

The board. Below, Doug, Griffith, Mary and Charlie signing the articles of incorporation

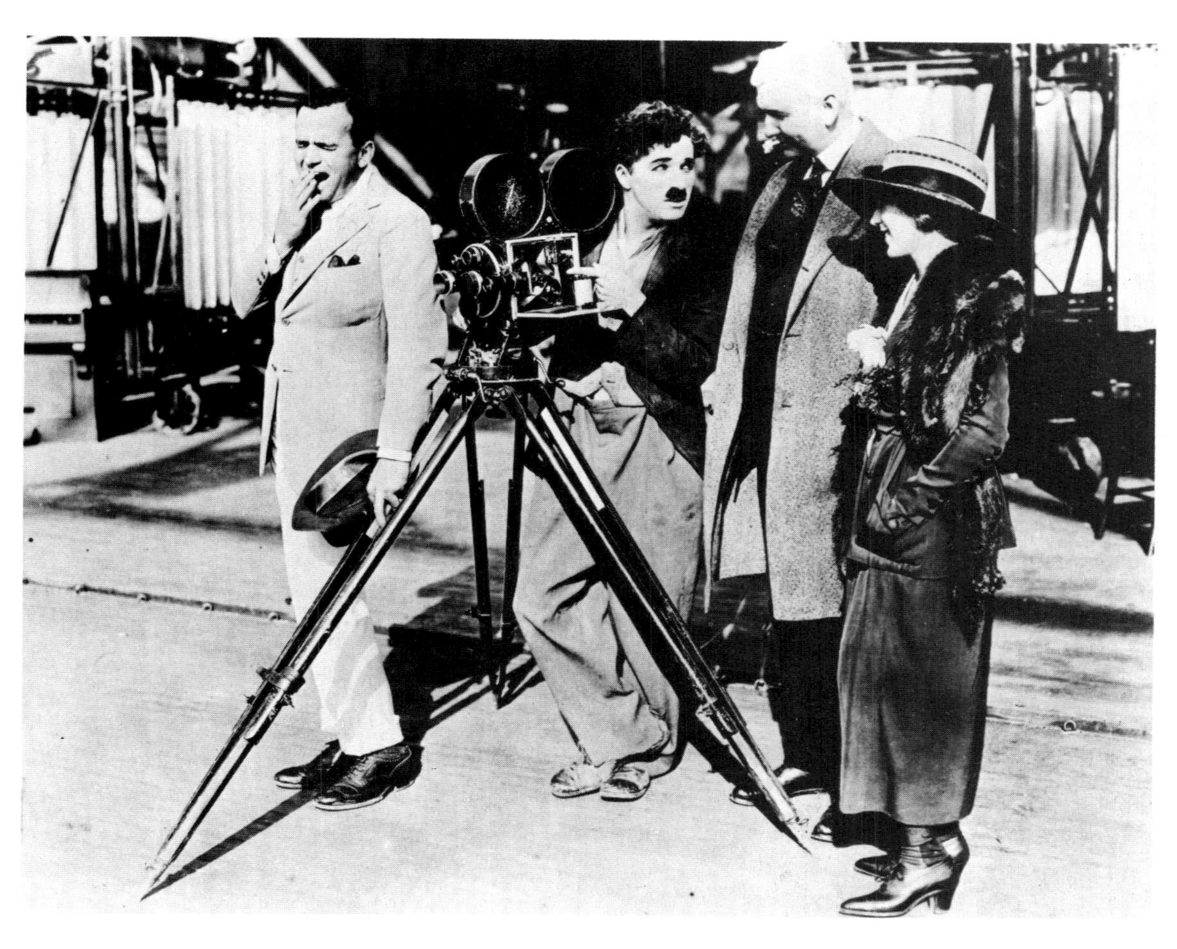

Work and play . . . with Doug Fairbanks

Author, but not on this occasion actor

For his first straight dramatic film, Chaplin concentrates on directing

A Woman of Paris

Above, directing Adolphe Menjou. Below, Edna as tragic actress

1 **A Woman of Paris**
2,450m (shot between November 1922 and September 1923, and first released 1 October 1923)
Director/Screenplay: Charles Chaplin. Assistant directors: Charles Riesner, Harry d'Abbadie d'Arrast. Photography: Rollie Totheroh, Jack Wilson. Art Director: Charles Hall. Production manager: Alfred Reeves. Cast: Edna Purviance, Adolphe Menjou, Carl Miller, Lydia Knott, Charles French, Clarence Geldert, Betty Morrissey, Malvina Polo, Karl Gutman, Nellie Bly Baker, Henry Bergman, Harry Northrup. With Charles Chaplin, as one of the extras.

Marie Saint-Clair is in love with Jean Millet. Leaving her fiancé to tend his dying father, she returns alone to Paris, where she becomes the mistress of the wealthy and cynical Pierre Revel. When she is reunited with Jean, his mother opposes their marriage. Jean cannot deal with these events and commits suicide. His mother plans to kill Marie in revenge, but the two women become friends, united by their devotion to the dead man.

A Woman of Paris

A Woman of Paris

Edna Purviance and Adolphe Menjou

A Woman of Paris

A Woman of Paris

Left, Edna Purviance, Carl Miller, Adolphe Menjou

A Woman of Paris

'*A Woman of Paris* was set in France, and to ensure that the atmosphere was authentic, Chaplin appealed for help to two good friends, Jean de Limur and Harry d'Abbadie d'Arrast. D'Arrast, as Chaplin's right-hand man, was generally in charge of production and research, while Jean de Limur, who also appeared in the film, was technical director.'

Robert Florey

Lydia Knott, Carl Miller, Edna Purviance

Brief encounters

After his divorce from Mildred Harris, and before he met Pola Negri, Chaplin had a brief flirtation with Claire Windsor

Pola Negri and the actor Charles de Rochefort

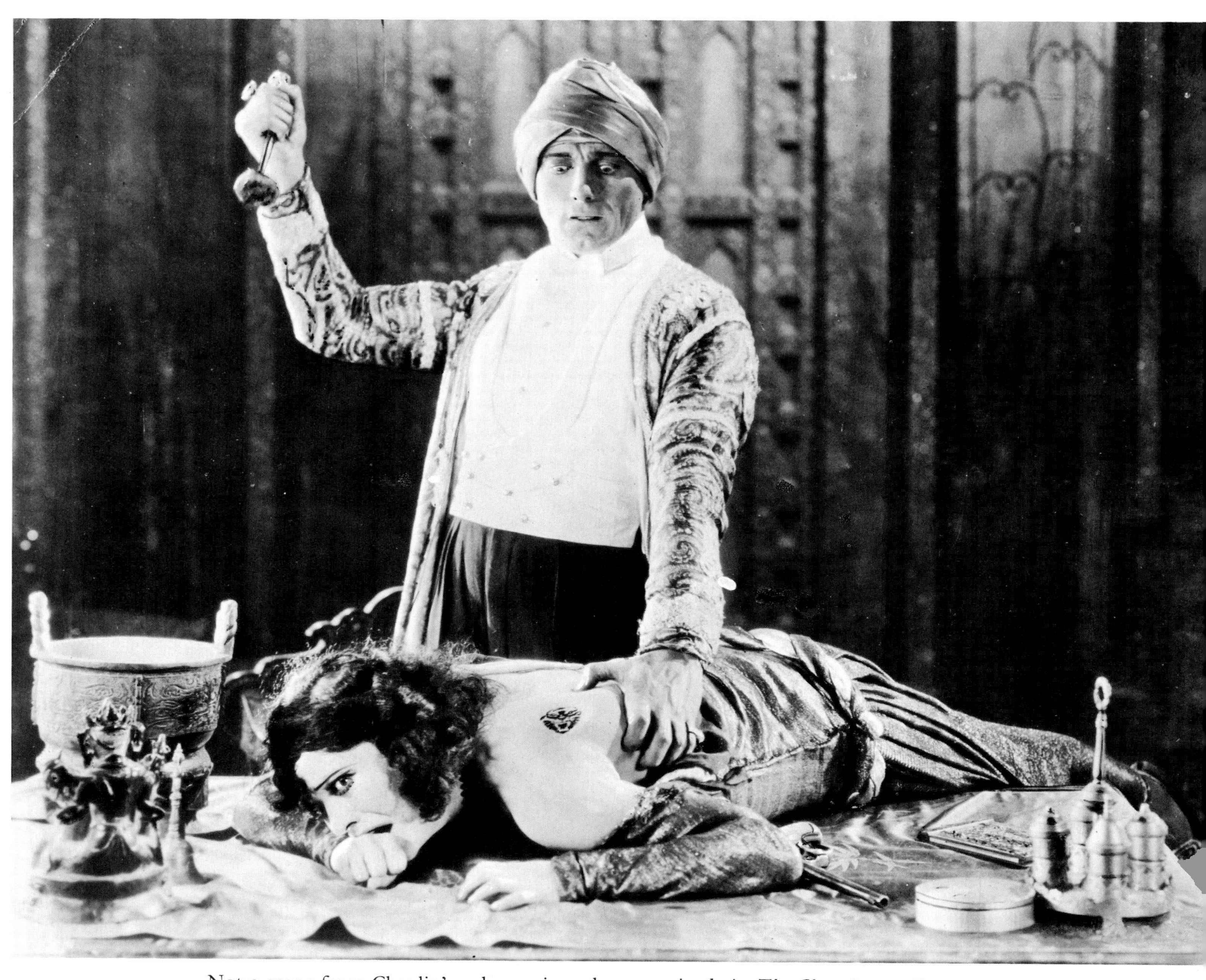

Not a scene from Chaplin's subconscious, but an episode in *The Cheat* (1923; George Fitzmaurice), starring Pola Negri

1925
The Gold Rush

2 **The Gold Rush**
First version: 3,129m; second version: 2,720m. Shot between January 1924 and May 1925. First released 26 June 1925. Sound version (2,150m) with added narration by Chaplin and music soundtrack: 6 March 1942.
Director/Screenplay: Charles Chaplin. Assistant directors: Charles Riesner, Harry d'Abbadie d'Arrast. Photography: Rollie Totheroh, Jack Wilson. Art director: Charles Hall. Production manager: Alfred Reeves. Cast: Charles Chaplin, Georgia Hale, Mack Swain, Tom Murray, Henry Bergman, Malcom Waite, Betty Morrissey

Charlie is a gold prospector in the Klondike in the early years of this century. He and Big Jim take refuge in the cabin belonging to Black Larsen, a villain. Larson returns, there's a fierce fight, but peace is restored. Larsen then goes out in the storm, kills two men and takes their dogs, and makes off.

In the meantime Charlie is dying of hunger and cooks up one of his boots. Big Jim has hallucinations and thinks Charlie is a delicious chicken . . . Charlie makes a dash for it, kills a bear and eats a proper meal, and arrives eventually in a mining town. At the saloon he falls madly in love with dancer Georgia. By a trick he gets the use of Hank's cabin, and there prepares a New Year's Eve dinner for Georgia and friends – having earned the money by sweeping snow.

But Georgia has forgotten her promise. Charlie sits facing two bread rolls, spears them with two forks – and the two little shoes perform a dance of waiting and despair. Big Jim shows up again. He's struck gold but forgotten where his concession is. He offers Charlie a half-share in return for his help. A storm blows the cabin on to the cliff edge but the two have a miraculous escape from death – and then find the claim that will make them millionaires. On the boat home, Charlie meets Georgia again. She thinks he's a stowaway and hides him. All is revealed and a happy ending ensues.

The Gold Rush

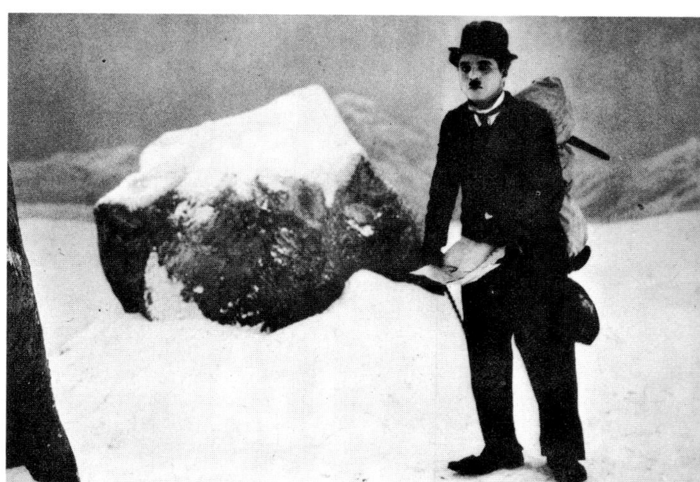

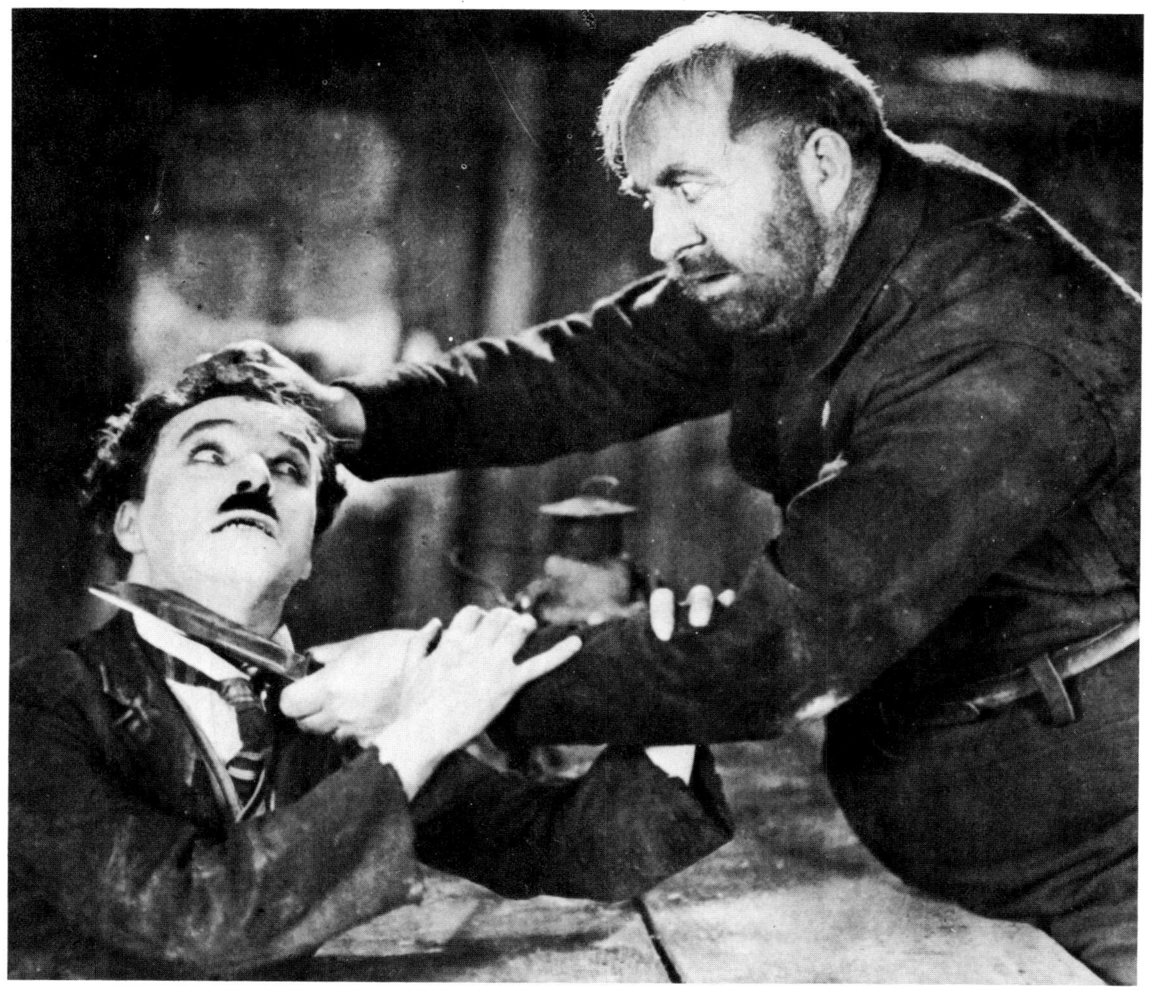

The Gold Rush

The Gold Rush

Chagall used this hallucination as the basis for a caricature of Chaplin (for René Schwob's *Une mélodie silencieuse*), in which he is shown with hen's feet and carrying wings (angel's wings) tucked underneath his arm (see page 407)

Below, boiling up a boot, and opposite, getting down to the pasta

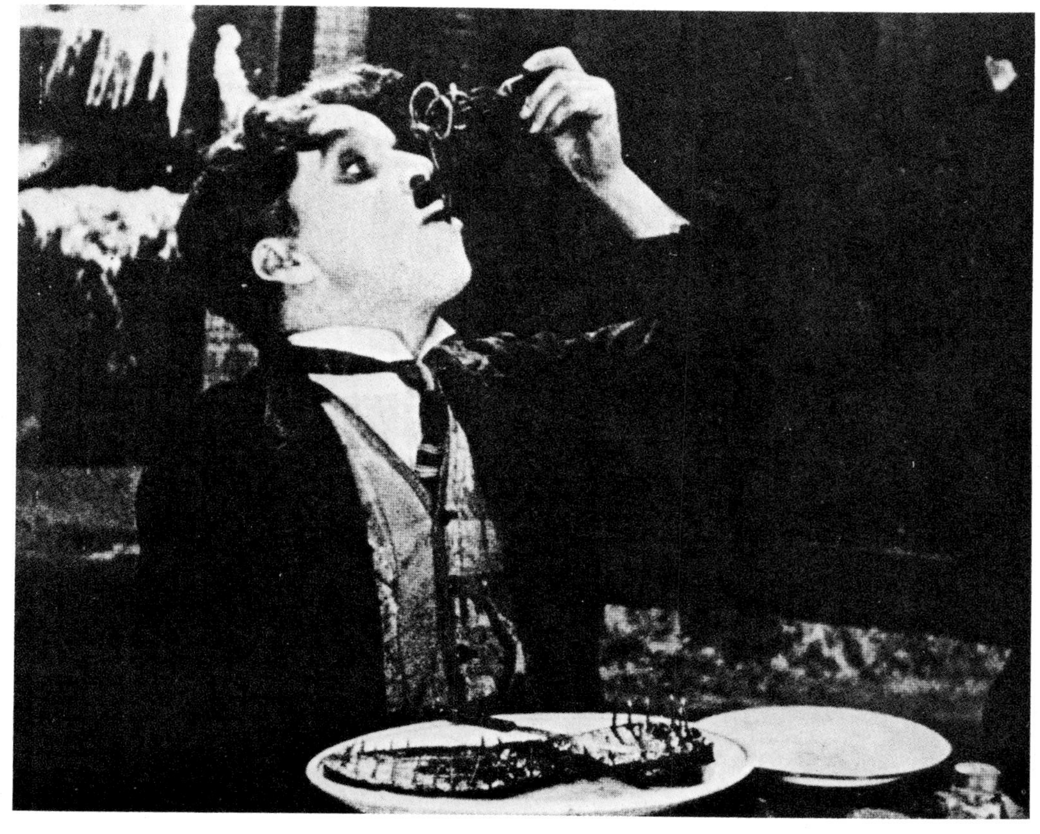

513L

The Gold Rush

'Every time he appears, I feel a sense of balance and sureness that allows my ideas to burgeon and frees my thought. He shows me what's in me. What's truest in me. Most human. For man to speak to man is rare, is it not?'

Elie Faure

HAPPY
NEW
YEAR

HAPPY
NEW
YEAR

The Gold Rush

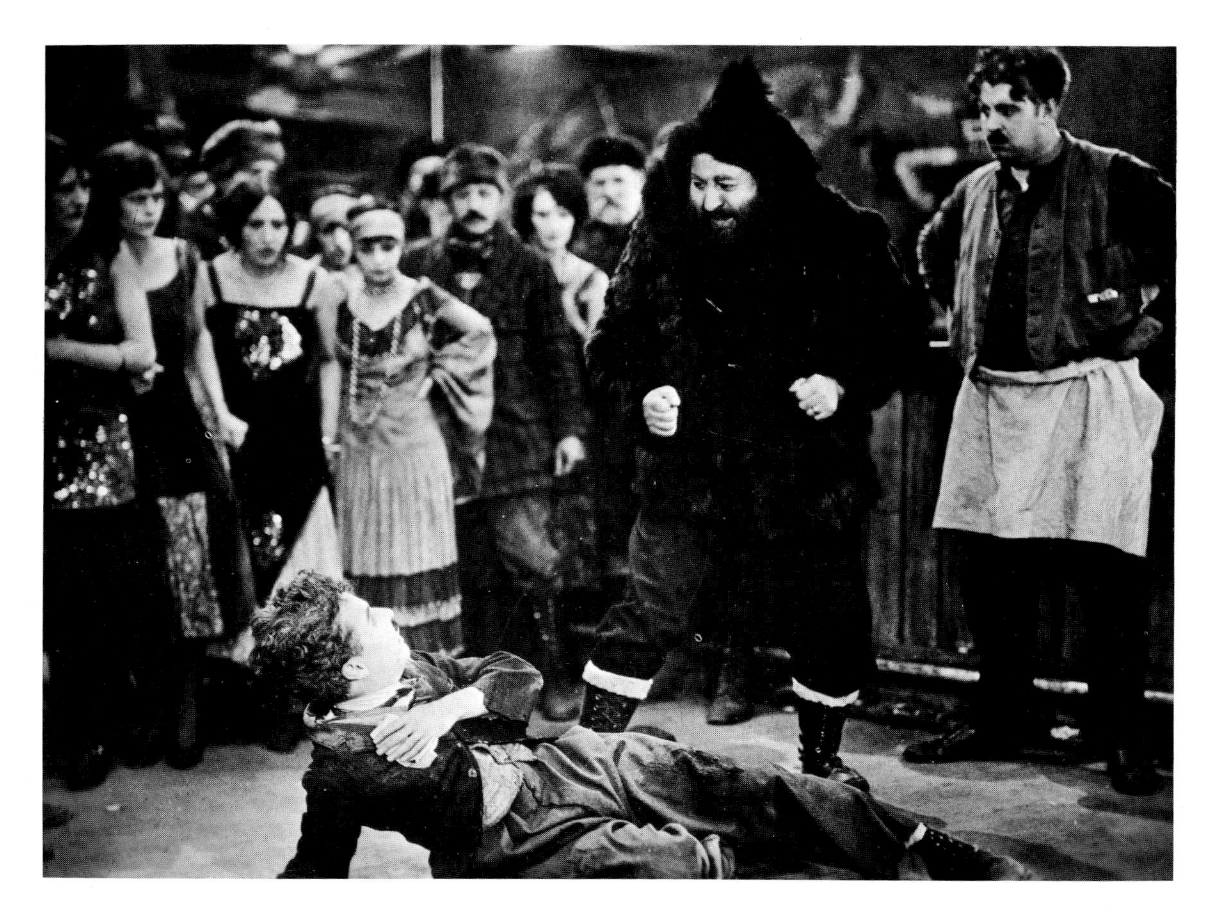

NEW
YEAR

12

The Gold Rush

'Long before he immortalized his "dance of the rolls" on the screen (right and overleaf), on many occasions when we lunched at Musso Frank's restaurant, Chaplin provided us with endless fun by draping a napkin round his neck like a curtain, spearing two rolls with forks and making them dance to the accompaniment of songs in the style of the Lancashire Lads.'

Robert Florey

The Gold Rush

The Gold Rush

The Gold Rush

Genius – ninety percent effort and painstaking preparation

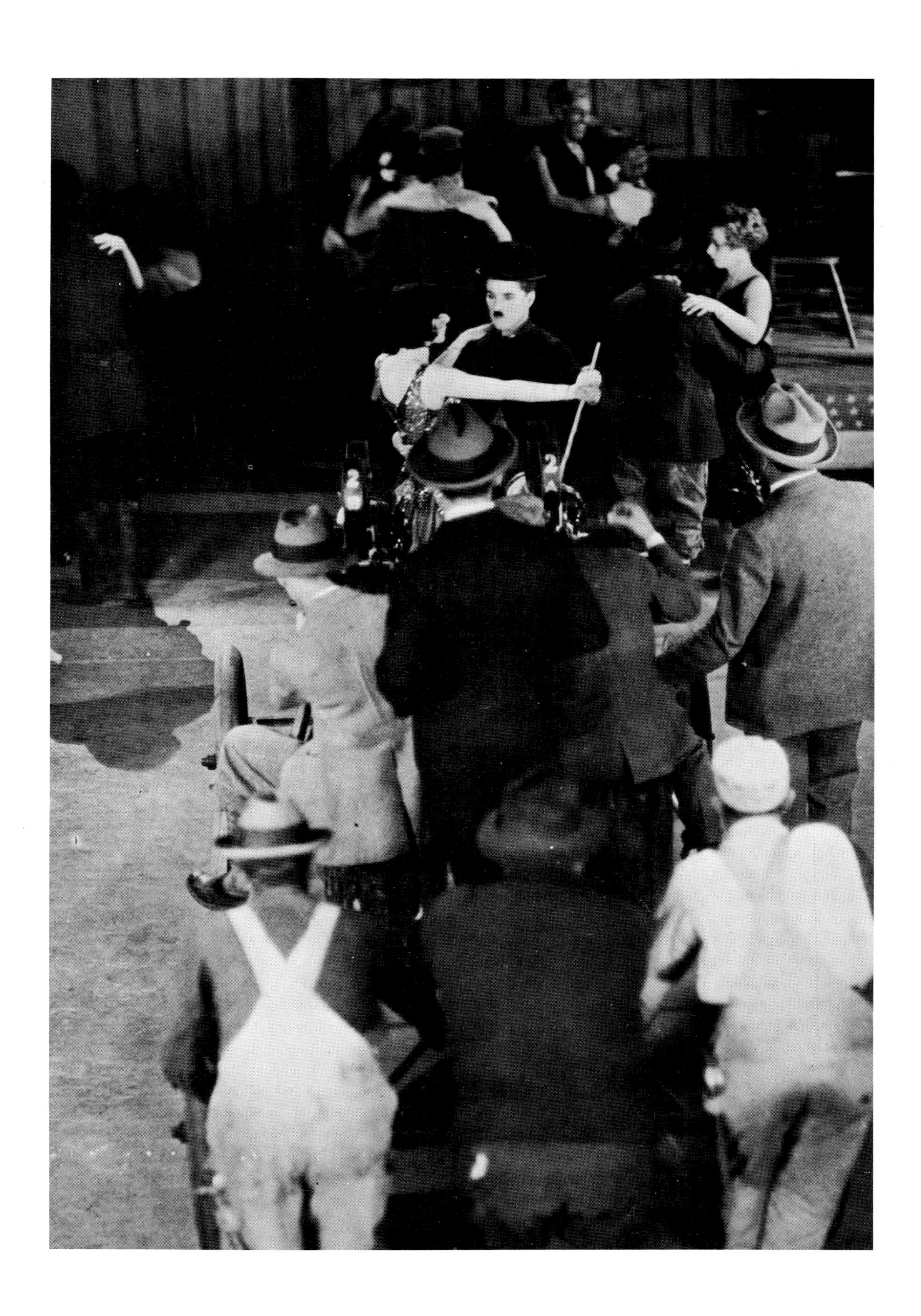

The dream factory from a different angle, during the arduous shooting of *The Gold Rush*

The Gold Rush

The Gold Rush

The Gold Rush

Georgia Hale and Chaplin, a real-life romance

Georgia Hale, for a time the leading lady in Chaplin's private life

Scandal

In November 1924, Chaplin had married Lita Grey in Mexico. He originally intended her to be his co-star in *The Gold Rush*. Their divorce, in late 1927, caused a huge scandal. By paying a million dollars Chaplin won custody of the two children

The divorce case sparked off a campaign of vilification in the press. One cartoonist at least acknowledged that the talent remained intact in spite of the mud-slinging

Chaplin had until now been resolutely silent

1942

The Gold Rush

Sound version

The Seagull

The Seagull (A Woman of the Sea)
Shot 1926. Never distributed.
Director: Josef von Sternberg. Photography: Paul Ivano. Art Director: Danny Hall. Continuity: Alice White. Cast: Edna Purviance, Eve Southern, Gayne Whitman, Guy Gillman.

Chaplin and his associates, Douglas Fairbanks, Mary Pickford and D.W. Griffith, had much admired Josef von Sternberg's *The Salvation Hunters*, with Georgia Hale; they bought the film and arranged distribution through United Artists. Chaplin then decided to produce von Sternberg's screenplay *The Seagull*, and asked him to direct it.

The Seagull

Location shooting in Monterey, with, left to right, the photographer Rozick, Edna Purviance, Paul Ivano, Alice White (then a continuity girl, later a star), von Sternberg (foreground, sitting on a rock), Eve Southern (wearing plaits) and Guy Gillman.

Production started in April 1926 in Chaplin's studios. The director of photography was Paul Ivano, an American cameraman, born in Nice in 1900, who had gone to Hollywood in 1919 and there worked in close association with Nazimova and Valentino. On this film he executed the longest tracking shot ever attempted in a Hollywood street. In a box on wheels pushed by technicians, he shot four hundred metres of film without a break, following the progress of an actor as he asks passers-by for money, sits down on a bench, picks up cigarette-ends and then takes a tramp's newspaper.

The film was shot in six weeks, and von Sternberg arranged a showing at the Beverly Hills Theatre. Robert Florey and Paul Ivano were both present, but no one thought to invite Chaplin. He was furious, and refused to distribute the film, even though he had invested $80,000 of his own money in the venture.

Rollie Totheroh later told Robert Florey that the negative of the film had not been destroyed and remained in Chaplin's archives. It was burned in 1933 for tax reasons.

The photographs reproduced, taken by Max Constant, are rare records of this production.

1928

The Circus

3 The Circus
2,124m (shot between October 1925 and October 1927; first released: 7 January 1928; sound version: 16 April 1969)
Director/Screenplay: Charles Chaplin. Assistant director: Harry Crocker. Photography: Rollie Totheroh, Jack Wilson, Mark Marklatt. Art director: Charles Hall; Assistant: William Hinckley. Music: Charles Chaplin. Musical arranger: P. Williamson.
Cast: Charles Chaplin, Merna Kennedy, Betty Morrissey, Harry Crocker, Allan Garcia, Henry Bergman, Stanley Sanford, George Davis, John Rand, Steve Murphy, Doc Stone, Albert Austin, Heinie Conklin.

Charlie is on the run from the police and stumbles into a circus. He's such a success that he is taken on as a clown. The bareback rider wins his heart, but he has a formidable rival in Rex, the tightrope walker. He can't outshine him either on the high wire or in Merna's eyes. When the circus leaves town, Charlie is left on the empty site with only his memories for company.

The Circus

The miracle of Charlie Chaplin is that he gave a sense of communion to people with widely differing viewpoints. He made whole hosts of people feel they understood one another, whereas in fact they were total strangers . . . He is, uniquely, cinema for all people – and for reasons that may on occasion seem contradictory.

Lucien Wahl

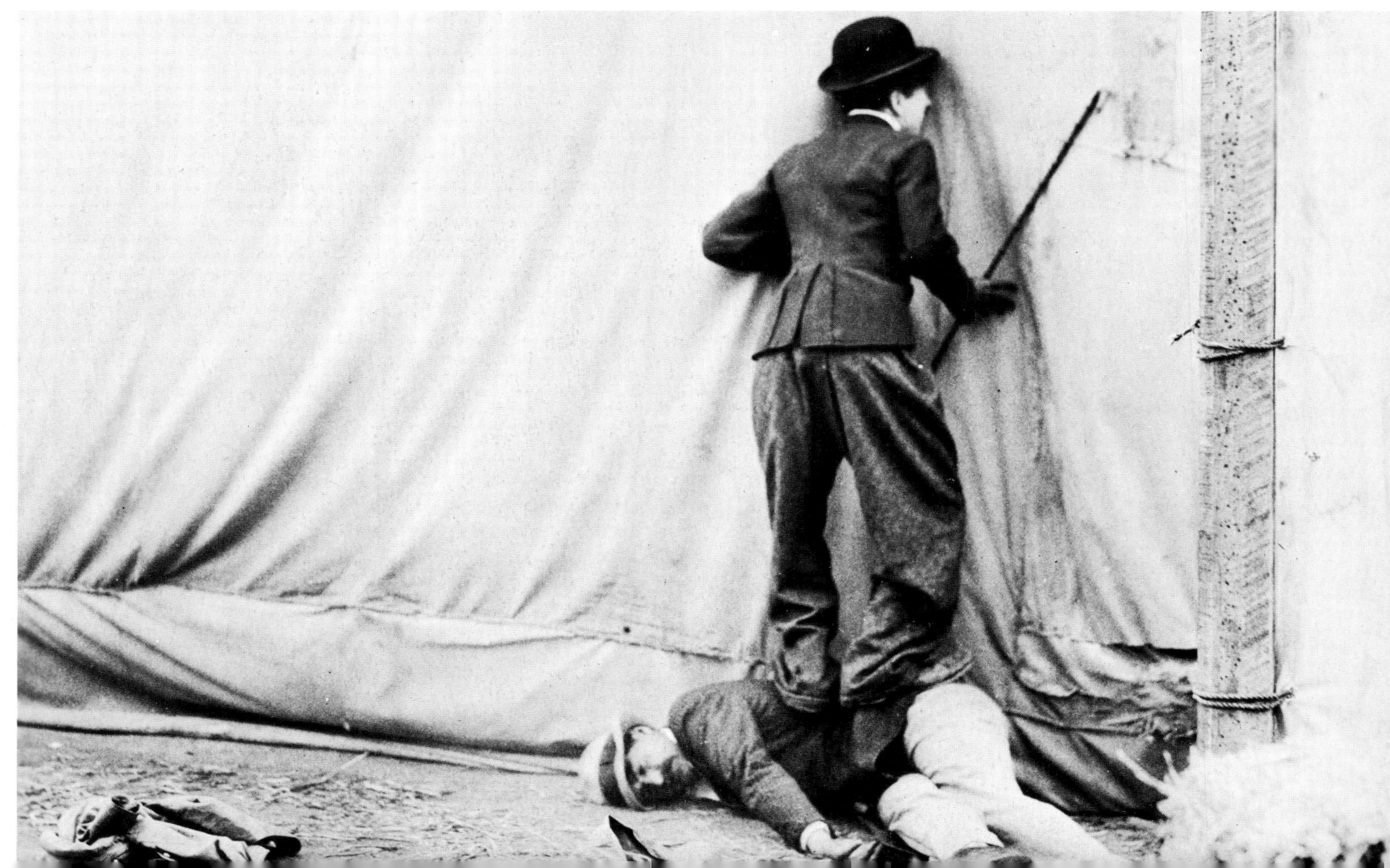

SALT WATER TAFFY
13

HAM

The Circus

Above, the best audience

The Circus

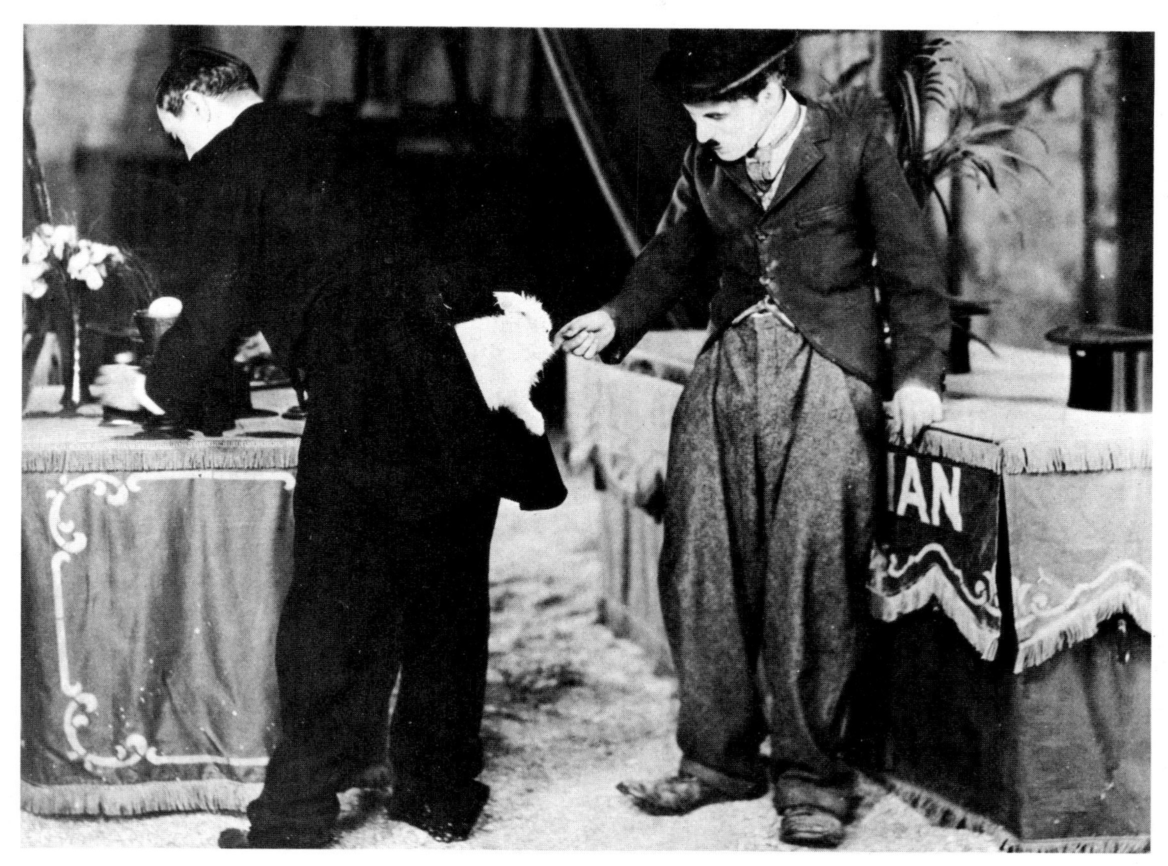

A discovery backstage . . . and in the ring

A cartload of talent . . .
. . . all to earn a modest crust

The Circus

The Circus

Magic misfires . . . the clown's fate

PROF. BOSCO
MAGICIAN

PRO
MA

The Circus

The Circus

'Chaplin is the modern Mr Punch. His appeal is to all ages, all people. Esperanto laughter. Everyone finds him entertaining for different reasons. With his help they would doubtless have finished the Tower of Babel.'

Jean Cocteau (1919)

The Circus

The Circus

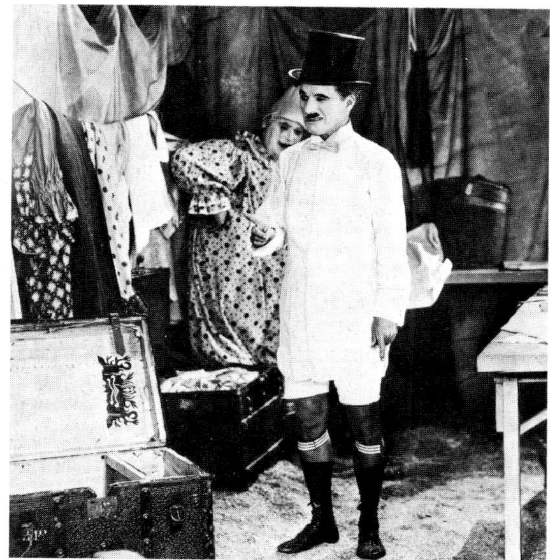

The Circus

The Circus

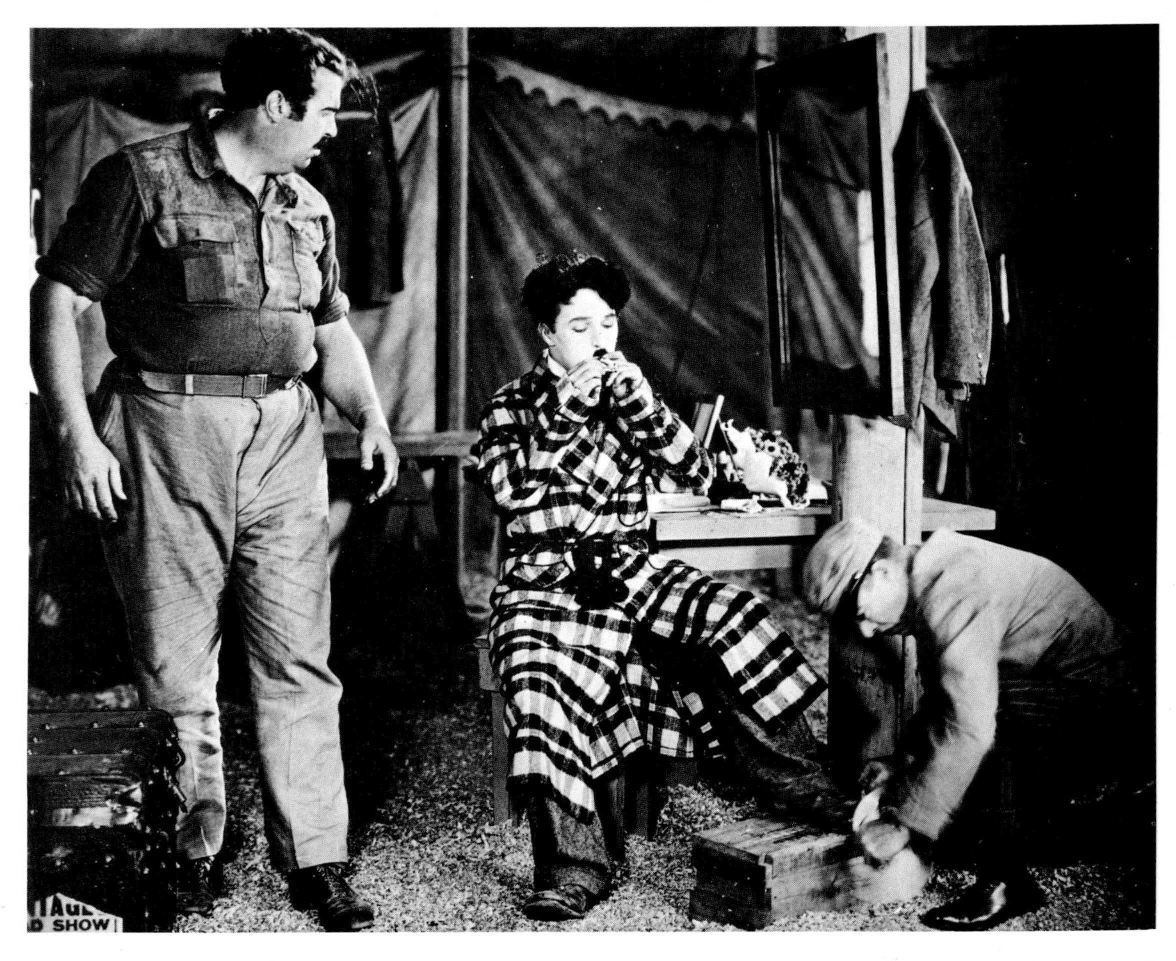

What the crowd doesn't see . . .

The actress Maude Kahler, known as Merna Kennedy (1908–44), was eighteen when Chaplin asked her to be his co-star in *The Circus*. In the divorce courts, Lita Grey accused her, without any evidence, of committing adultery with her husband. Merna Kennedy married the director Busby Berkeley in 1934.

1931

1931
City Lights

4 **City Lights**
2,380m (shot between June 1928 and December 1930, and first released 30 January 1931)
Director/Screenplay: Charles Chaplin. Assistant Directors: Harry Crocker, Henry Bergman, Albert Austin. Photography: Rollie Totheroh, Gordon Pollock, Mark Marklatt. Art Director: Charles Hall. Music: Charles Chaplin, orchestrated by Arthur Johnston. Cast: Charles Chaplin, Virginia Cherrill, Harry Myers, Hank Mann, Florence Lee, Allan Garcia, Eddie Baker, Henry Bergman, Albert Austin, James Donnelly, Robert Parrish, John Rand, Stanhope Wheatcroft, Jean Harlow (appearing as an extra).

The tender-hearted tramp, without a roof over his head, befriends a blind flower-seller and falls in love.

Because he saves a millionaire from drowning, he is given the use of his Rolls Royce and his mansion. The flower-girl is dazzled by this rich gentleman. When she falls ill, Charlie takes every job he can to ensure that she is cared for. He even persuades the millionaire to pay for an operation to restore her sight. But Charlie is accused of stealing the money and ends up in prison. A free man again, he passes by the shop-window of the beautiful florist. She looks with pity at the ragged fellow, gives him a rose and a coin, and, as she touches him, recognizes her benefactor . . .

City Lights

City Lights

Charlie's glimpse of heaven

City Lights

Love is blind

City Lights

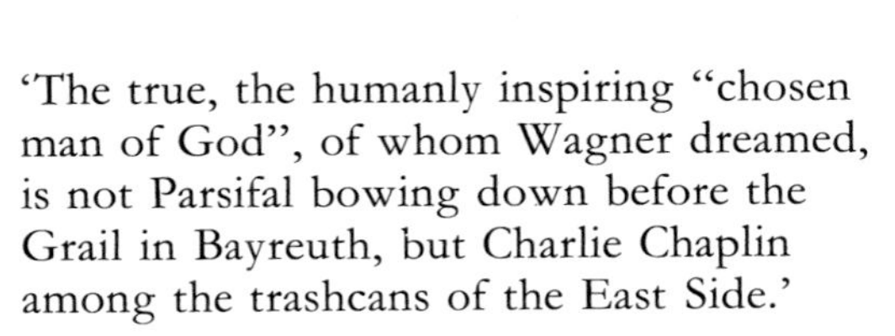

'The true, the humanly inspiring "chosen man of God", of whom Wagner dreamed, is not Parsifal bowing down before the Grail in Bayreuth, but Charlie Chaplin among the trashcans of the East Side.'

Sergei Eisenstein

City Lights

City Lights

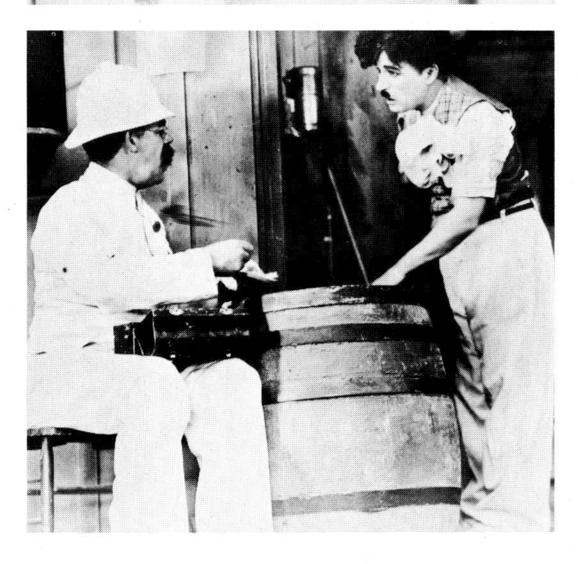

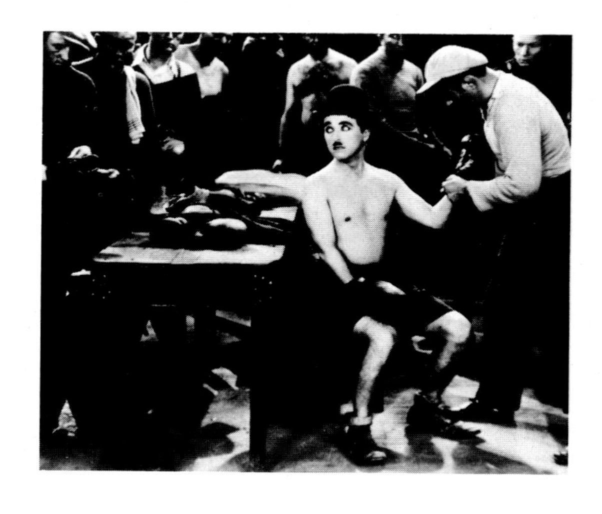

Shades of the old Keystone and Essanay shorts

EXIT

The flower of youth

Virginia Cherrill was barely twenty, and a socialite, when Chaplin encountered her at a boxing match and signed her to play the blind flower-seller in *City Lights*. Working with her on the set was not without its problems, and Charlie several times contemplated replacing her, but he was always swayed in the end by her beauty and youth.

Virginia Cherrill married five times, and from 1933 to 1935 was the wife of Cary Grant.

Chaplin with May Reeves. In her book, *Charlie Chaplin intime*, the acrobatic dancer gave a frank account of her holiday romance with Chaplin in Juan-les-Pins in 1931. Below, Chaplin, May Reeves and Emil Ludwig

Honours

Awarded the Legion of Honour. Place de la Concorde, Paris, 1931. It was not until 1975 that Chaplin received a knighthood and became Sir Charles Spencer Chaplin

The great and the powerful: with George Bernard Shaw, Winston Churchill, Albert Einstein

Above, Chaplin in the company of Gandhi. Below, leisure pursuits: riding with Colonel Hunter, private secretary to the Duke of Westminster, and tennis at Biarritz in 1931

True fame: the caricature

With his reputation as the greatest mime-artist of the century, Chaplin was seized upon by cartoonists as perfect material: at top left, Charlie Chaplin as seen by Gino Bolla (a card for an Italian film club); at bottom left, by Cabrol; at top right, by Garretto (hitherto unpublished); at bottom right, by Joe Bridge. At centre left, Chaplin as seen by himself!

And now epic glory

In 1929, the painter Charles de Ravennes executed a Napoleonic fresco that incorporated many of the Hollywood greats; Mary Pickford is to be seen giving succour to a distressed priest . . .

An idea for a film . . . or just a love of dressing up?

1935

Left, Chaplin in 1935. Above, his luxurious home in Beverly Hills, and below, with Paulette Goddard who became his wife in 1936

Paulette Goddard

Marion Levy, known as Paulette Goddard, was born in 1911, became a Ziegfield Follies girl at the age of fourteen, married a rich industrialist in 1931 and divorced soon afterwards. She went to Hollywood in 1932. Chaplin was bowled over by her and they were married during a trip to the Far East in 1936. After they were divorced in 1942, Paulette married Burgess Meredith, and later Erich Maria Remarque.

Paulette Goddard sketched by Chaplin

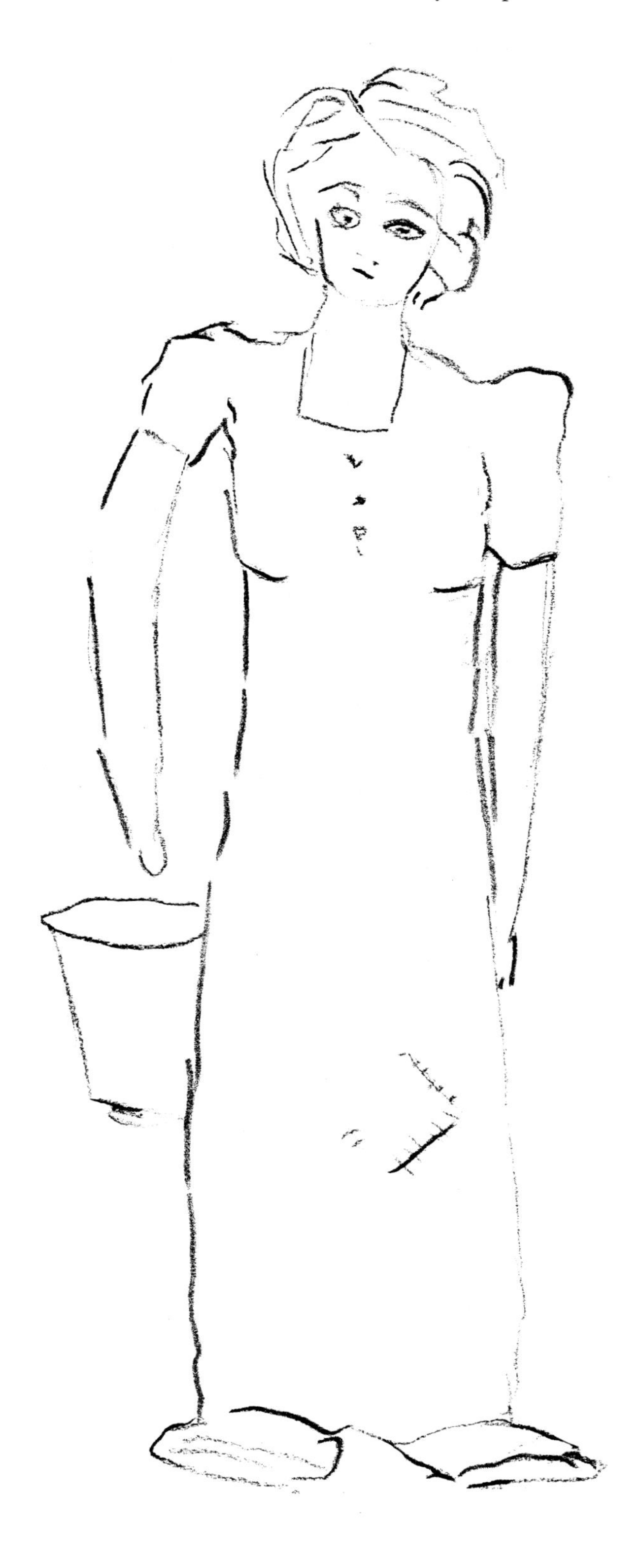

At Ensenada

The couple with Robert Florey

Visiting Angkor-Vat

Dea ex machina

Charlie the Tramp looks a happy man

5 **Modern Times**
2,320m (shot between October 1934 and September 1935, and first released 5 February 1936)
Director/Screenplay: Charles Chaplin. Assistant directors: Carter de Haven, Henry Bergman. Photography: Rollie Totheroh, Ira Morgan. Art director: Charles Hall; Assistant: Russell Spencer. Music: Charles Chaplin; arranged and directed by Alfred Newman, Edgar Powell, David Raksin. Cast: Charles Chaplin, Paulette Goddard, Hank Mann, Henry Bergman, Chester Conklin, Stanley Sanford, Louis Natheaux, Allan Garcia, Richard Alexander, Heinie Conklin, Lloyd Ingraham, Edward Kimball, Wilfred Lucas, Myra McKinney, John Rand, Walter James, Dr Cecil Reynolds.

Working on a factory conveyer-belt, Charlie is condemned to screw nuts on bolts all day long. A victim in every sense, he is sucked into a fearsome machine full of turning cog wheels. He goes beserk and is sent to a mental clinic. Back on the streets, with no job, he gets entangled with a red flag and is promptly arrested. Released from prison, he helps a pretty waif who has stolen some bread – and is promptly put back inside. But he escapes with the girl and they create an idyll in a wooden hut. Charlie gets a job as nightwatchman in a big store – and spends a wonderful night there with his girl. Rather than face prison again, the two leave the city and set off on the open road.

1936
Modern Times

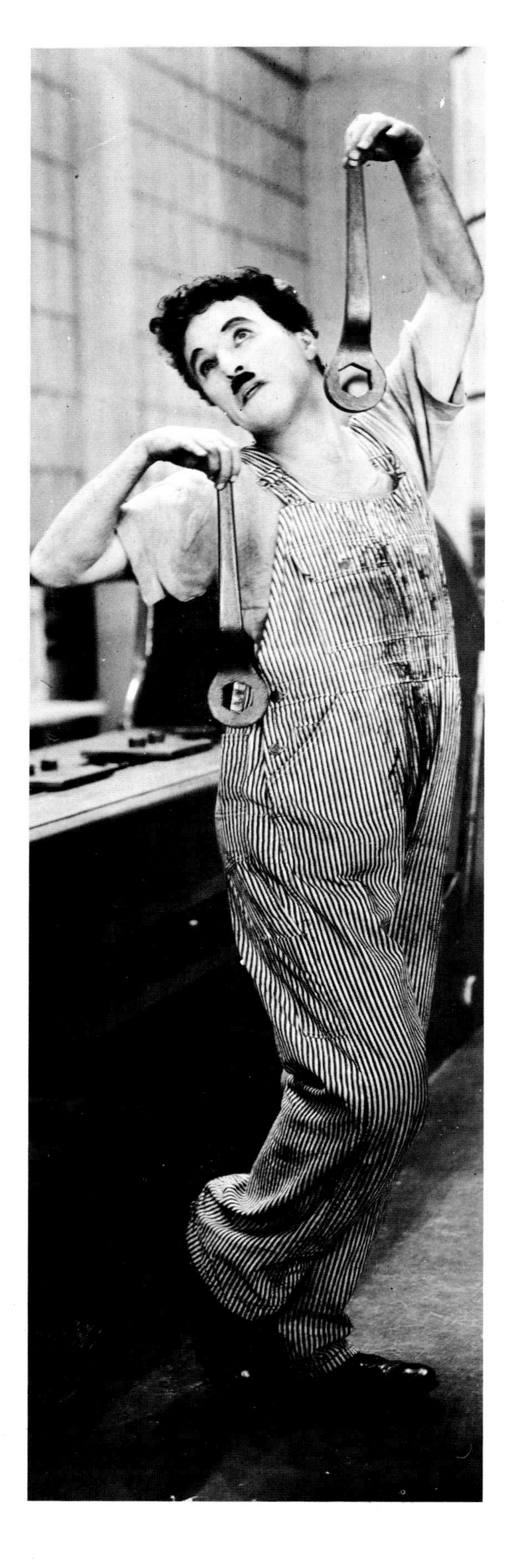

Flying the wrong flag

The streets of London are for Chaplin the scene of frolic, gaiety and extravagant adventure. They had a reality that the grandest well-tended avenues, with their rows of rich houses, could never possess. 'I can imagine him going into his own house and wondering what on earth he is doing in this strange man's dwelling.'

Somerset Maugham

Modern Times

The devil in the machine . . .

One fantastic night

Charlie the floorwalker

Modern Times

PLEASE
KNOCK
OUT
OF
ORDER

Still on the open road

Still on the open road, Chaplin, a happy man, is eager to share his good fortune with Charlie the Tramp

Unusually, Chaplin agreed to be photographed with an actress who did not appear in his films. She was Thelma Todd, whose beauty and wit made her a popular comedienne; in 1935, only a few months after this picture was taken, she was found dead in her car, asphyxiated by carbon monoxide fumes.

In 1940 in *The Great Dictator*, Chaplin returns to scenes reminiscent of *Shoulder Arms* (1918)

Chaplin was born in the same year as Adolf Hitler

In November 1938, the Nazis staged an exhibition in Munich called 'The Eternal Jew', in which a photograph of Chaplin appeared with the caption: 'An Englishman? No, a Jew.' In December 1938, Charlie began filming *The Great Dictator*.

1940
The Great Dictator

6 **The Great Dictator**
Talking picture, 3,420m (shot between September 1939 and January 1940; first released in New York: 15 October 1940)
Director/Screenplay: Charles Chaplin. Assistant directors: Henry Bergman, Dan James, Wheeler Dryden, Bob Meltzer. Photography: Rollie Totheroh, Karl Strauss. Art Director: J. Russell Spencer. Music: Charles Chaplin. Music Director: Meredith Wilson.
Cast: Charlie Chaplin, Jack Oakie, Reginald Gardiner, Billy Gilbert, Henry Daniell, Grace Hayle, Carter de Haven, Paulette Goddard, Emma Dunn, Maurice Moscovitch, Bernard Gorcey, Paul Weigel, Hank Mann, Chester Conklin, Esther Michelson, Florence Wright, Eddie Gribbon, Robert O. Davis, Eddie Dunn, Peter Lynn, Nita Pike, Richard Alexander, Lucien Prival, Leo White.

The little Jewish barber who lives in the ghetto is the double of the mighty dictator who wants to exterminate the Jews. He is arrested, together with one of the dictator's aides who has changed sides. Meanwhile Hannah, the girl from the ghetto whom the barber has protected, manages to escape to a neighbouring country, and the two men escape from a concentration camp. The dictator, while entertaining another dictator with whom he hopes to make an alliance, is arrested by his own guards, who mistake him for the escapee; the barber takes his place and delivers to his astonished people a message of peace and humanity.

The Great Dictator

The Great Dictator

The dignified calm of the Chancellory . . .
It is here that the orders for extermination
are issued

The Great Dictator

A humble milieu . . . the little man at his work

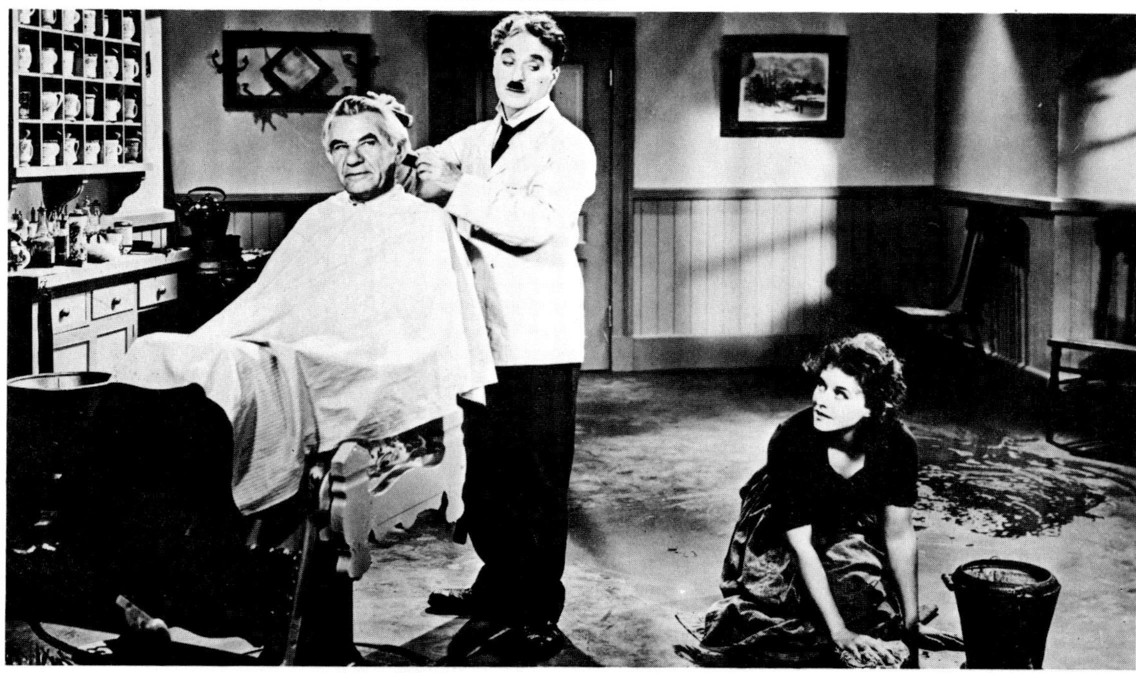

The Great Dictator

The Great Dictator

The Great Dictator

Dreaming of a place in history . . . and a Thousand Years of Power

The Great Dictator

Surrounded by buffoons . . .

The Great Dictator

In place of the double-headed eagle, Chaplin invented the eagle with three feet

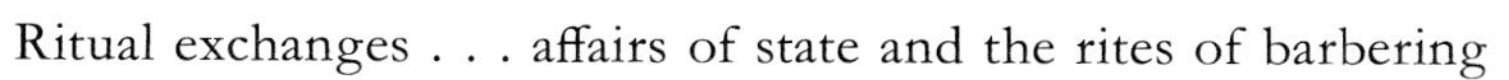

Ritual exchanges . . . affairs of state and the rites of barbering

Again, the dance

Rural repose

The Great Dictator

It's strange . . . two dictators keep returning to the word LIBERTY

A happy marriage

On 16 June 1943 Chaplin married Oona O'Neill (above and below right), daughter of Eugene O'Neill. She was then eighteen, born in 1925 when Chaplin was shooting *The Gold Rush*

The age of love and friendship: below left, with Orson Welles

Oona portrayed as wife and mother; Charlie Chaplin is seen framed in the background

Three children . . .

Family life

Hollywood, above; the moustache is real.
Right, Return to London

Below, a family portrait. Left to right: Josephine, Charlie, Geraldine, Michael, and, in Oona's arms, the youngest child, Victoria

1947

Monsieur Verdoux

7 **Monsieur Verdoux**
Talking picture. 123 minutes (shot between May and September 1946, and first released 11 April 1947)
Director/Screenplay: Charles Chaplin; from an idea by Orson Welles. Associate director: Robert Florey. Assistant director: Wheeler Dryden. Photography: Rollie Totheroh, Curt Courant, Wallace Chewing. Art Director: John Beckman. Costumes: Drew Tetrick. Music: Charles Chaplin. Music director and arranger: Rudolph Schrager. Cast: Charles Chaplin, Mady Correll, Allison Roddell, Robert Lewis, Audrey Betz, Martha Raye, Isobel Elsom, Margaret Hoffman, Ada-May, Helene Heigh, Marjorie Bennett, Marilyn Nash, Irving Bacon, Virginia Brissac, Edwin Mills, Almira Sessions, Eula Morgan, Bernard Nedell, Charles Evans, William Frawley, Arthur Hohl, Fritz Leiber, Barbara Slater, John Harmon, Vera Marshe, Christine Ell, Lois Conklin, Pierre Watkin, Tom Wilson, Wheeler Dryden, Phillip Smalley, Barry Norton, Edna Purviance.

Monsieur Verdoux is a bank clerk, but when he loses his job he assumes many other identities. To him crime is a simple business transaction. In order to make adequate provision for his wife and son, he incinerates, poisons and slaughters women whom he has first taken the precaution of 'marrying', so that he can prudently invest the money he inherits.

Years later, a widower in reduced circumstances, he gives himself up, and before submitting to the death penalty, makes an impassioned attack on society.

Orson Welles supplied Chaplin with the original idea for a film based on the notorious French mass-murderer Landru, who was guillotined in 1922. Chaplin was also influenced by a still photograph from a German film (unspecified), which made a strong impression on him.

Monsieur Verdoux

Photo Robert Florey

In *Monsieur Verdoux*, Chaplin shows more than ever a meticulous attention to the detail of directing a picture, planning and sketching the scenes in advance.

Below, his previously unpublished drawings of a street corner in the town where the action is set, and for the attempted-drowning scene

'Café des Boulevards': an anonymous passerby in an anonymous street

Monsieur Verdoux

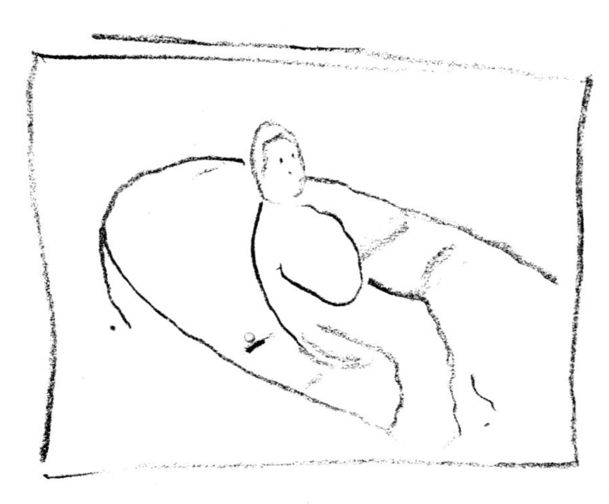

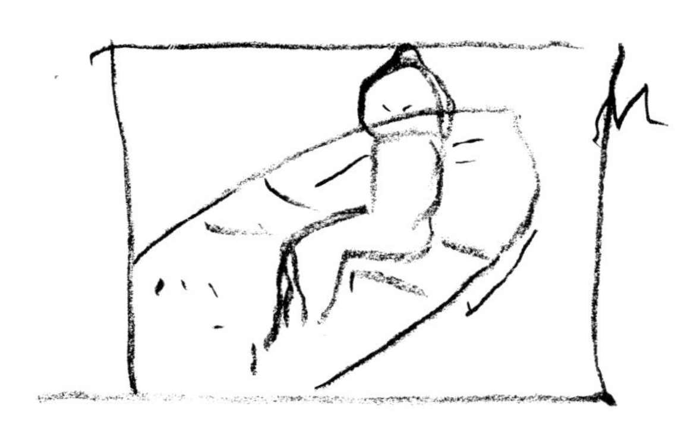

Chaplin's previously unpublished sketches

Monsieur Verdoux

In a split-second piece of comedy timing, it is the murderer who falls into the water. Other scenes shot on location at Arrowhead Lake, in the San Bernardino Mountains, appear on p.360

ANNA: What do you know about business?

VERDOUX: Emphatically more than you do, my dear.

ANNA: The last time you were home you came barging in here, telling me all the banks were going ~~to close. go broke~~ broke.

(CLOSE UP OF VERDOUX - Annabella's voice coming over)

2 X ~~Getting me all~~ horsed up about ~~taking my~~ money ~~out~~. It's a good job I didn't!

VERDOUX: Very well then, we'll forget it.

ANNA: Now don't get mad.

VERDOUX: (with quiet dignity) I'm not mad, ~~my dear~~ Annabella. I'm merely trying to save you from squandering ~~your money~~ on these ~~worthless enterprises~~.

ANNA: They're not all worthless.

VERDOUX: All of them.

ANNA: I still have faith in the Pacific Ocean Power Company.

VERDOUX: Good heavens! ... another one?

1 X what little money you have left on these ridiculous — stocks that are worthless.

2 X getting me all hornswoggled up about bringing my money home here. It's a good job I didn't!

Wives and victims

Wives and victims, of every shape and kind: (top) Almira Sessions, Ada-May, Mady Correll, Isobel Elsom; (bottom) Margaret Hoffman, Virginia Brissac, Helene Heigh and Barbara Slater, the pretty florist

Marilyn Nash, the youngest and the most surprising of the 'wives', and, right, the seducer

Monsieur Verdoux

The Arc de Triomphe ornament . . .

The sweet music of rustling banknotes . . .

Above, the Vendôme ornament among the lady's antiques

What could be more innocent than a cabin trunk?

A decent man . . . a big café . . . a good place for a secret rendezvous

Morrow the detective (production sketch by Charles Chaplin)

Monsieur Verdoux

A tendency towards misogyny is never more clearly expressed than in these sketches for hats

Of the first water . . .

Needs must

Monsieur Verdoux

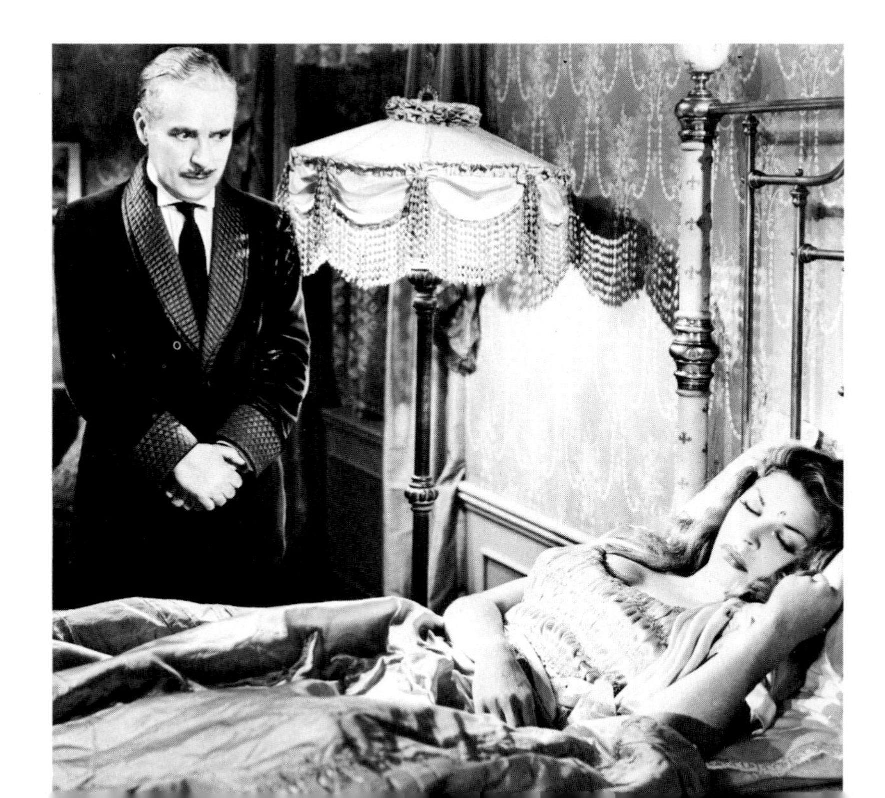

Monsieur Verdoux

Fatal gesture

Monsieur Verdoux

Marilyn Nash and kitten

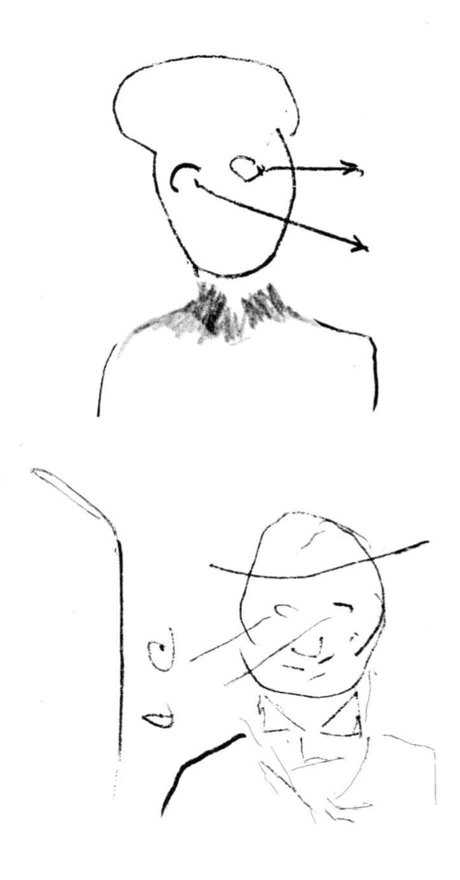

Unpublished sketches

Monsieur Verdoux

No harm in an exchange of glances

Though dealing with murder, the film was conceived of as comedy by Chaplin, who sketched a sample credit title, below

The end of the road

Monsieur Verdoux

Chaplin asked Robert Florey to be his associate director as the film was set in France. 'An unforgettable experience,' declared Florey (left, below). The director of photography, Rollie Totheroh (left), had worked with Chaplin for thirty-five years and was a devoted friend and colleague

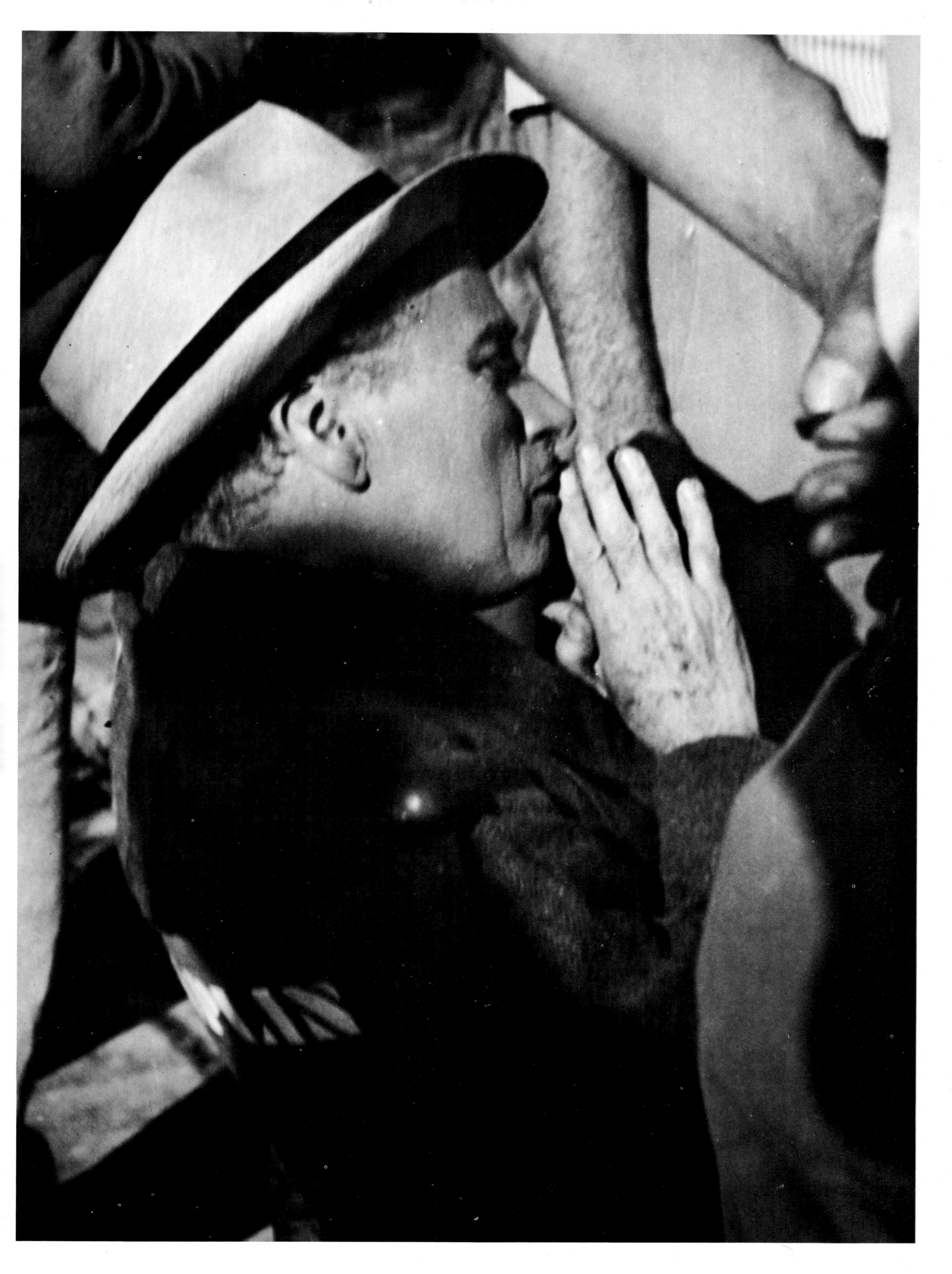

Monsieur Verdoux

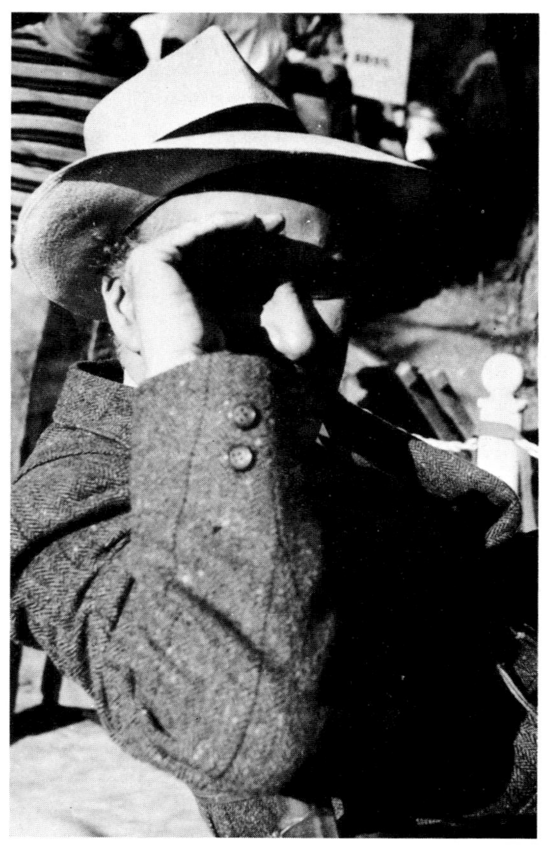

Left, on location. Above, 'Monsieur Verdoux' turns to that early genius of the French cinema, Méliès

In 1947, not long after the release of *Monsieur Verdoux*, the author visited Chaplin at his home (above and below), and heard of his desire to leave the United States

Monsieur Verdoux was unfavourably received by the American press; Chaplin was attacked and accused of 'un-American activities'. It was years before he made another film. He lived in memories of the past. Right: a drawing of 1899 by Phil May; and below right, the silent-comedy world of Charlie the tramp; below, Charlie Chaplin in the manner of Whistler, by John Decker

The part of the doctor was played by Wheeler Dryden, Chaplin's half-brother

1952
Limelight

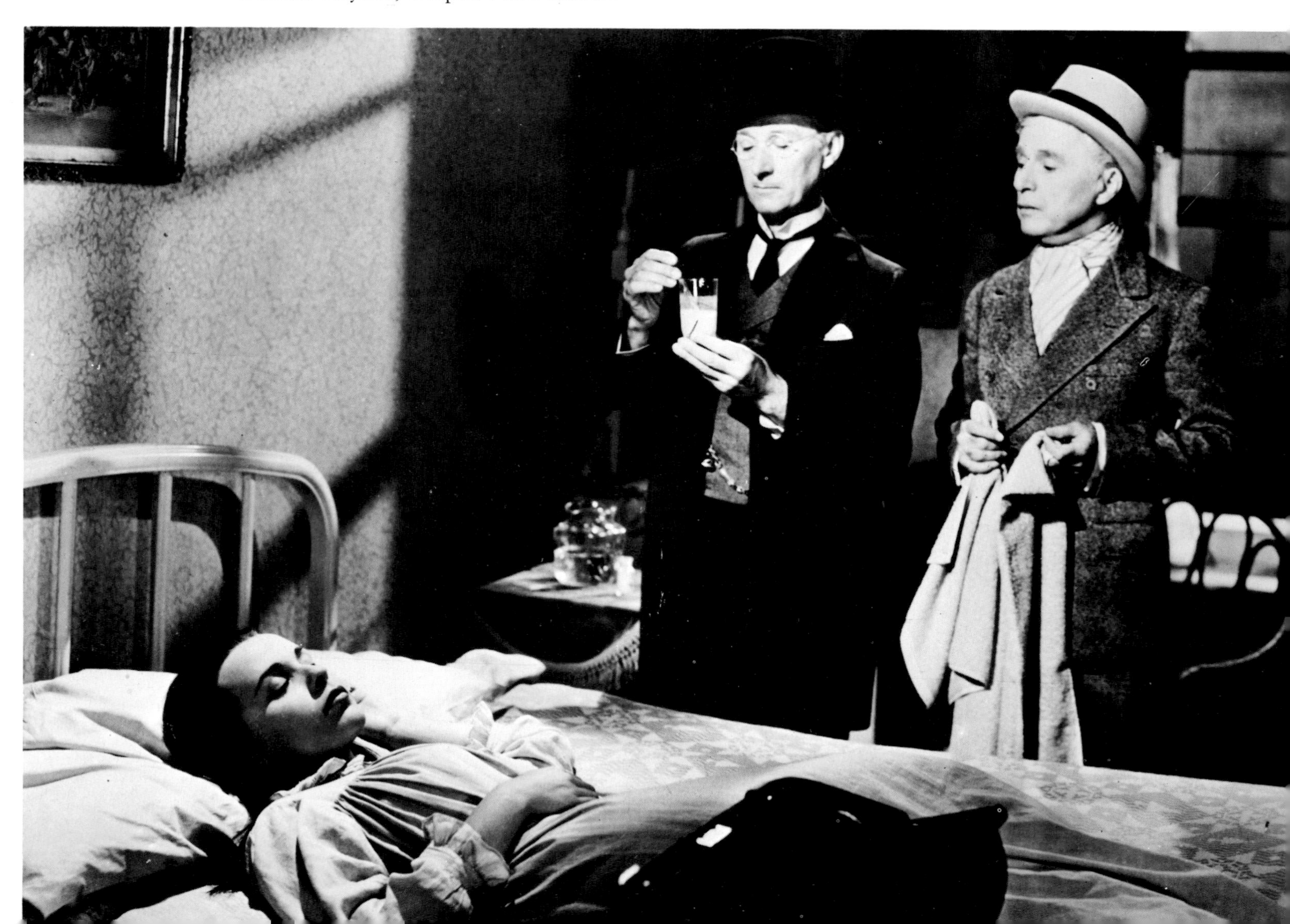

Limelight

8 **Limelight**
Talking picture. 143 minutes (shot between October 1951 and January 1952, and first released 16 October 1952)
Director/Screenplay: Charles Chaplin. Assistant directors: Robert Aldrich, Wheeler Dryden, Jerry Epstein. Photography: Karl Strauss, Rollie Totheroh. Art director: Eugene Lourie. Editor: Joe Inge. Music/choreography: Charles Chaplin. Assistant musical director: Ray Rasch. Cast: Charles Chaplin, Claire Bloom, Sydney Chaplin, Nigel Bruce, Norman Lloyd, Buster Keaton, Marjorie Bennett, Wheeler Dryden, Barry Bernard, Stapleton Kent, Mollie Blessing, Leonard Mudie, Julian Ludwig, Snub Pollard, Loyal Underwood, Edna Purviance, Geraldine Chaplin, Michael Chaplin, Josephine Chaplin, André Eglevsky, Melissa Hayden, Charles Chaplin Jr.

Calvero, a former star of the music halls, saves a young dancer, whose legs are paralyzed, from suicide. He cares for her and, to earn money for her, stages a comeback – but flops. The girl makes such strenuous efforts to console him that her paralysis is suddenly cured. She becomes a ballerina and lives with a young composer, and later organizes a benefit gala for Calvero. After a triumphant evening, the old man falls into the orchestra pit and dies, with a smile on his lips.

Limelight

A London street – the three young extras are Chaplin's children

Below, bowler hat and walking-stick – the only allusions to Charlie the Tramp

Limelight

Limelight

Chaplin with his son Sydney

Below, with Buster Keaton (1895-1966)

Two Independent Productions (1957–67)

1 **A King in New York**
Talking picture. 105 minutes (shot in Great Britain between 7 May and 28 July 1957, and first released in London: 12 September 1957)
Director/Screenplay: Charles Chaplin. Photography: Georges Périnal. Art Director: Alan Harris. Editor: John Seabourne. Music: Charles Chaplin. Production company: Attica Films. Cast: Charles Chaplin, Dawn Addams, Oliver Johnston, Michael Chaplin, Maxine Audley, Jerry Desmonde, Phil Brown, Harry Green, John McLaren, Alan Gifford, Shani Wallis, Joy Nichols, Joan Ingram, Sidney James, George Woodbridge, Robert Arden, Lauri Lupino Lane, George Truzzi.

King Shahdov of Estrovia is deposed. He arrives in New York, and his beautiful neighbour decides he can be exploited in TV commercials – for deodorants, whisky, rejuvenating creams, etc. When Shahdov befriends a boy whose parents are under investigation for 'un-American activities', he too is called before the Committee. Cleared, he flees to Europe to escape the hysteria that has overtaken the nation.

1957
A King in New York

A King in New York

A King in New York

A King in New York

Chaplin's work is accomplished, as director, actor, mime, composer and producer. He has become a legend in his lifetime. No one can counterfeit Charlie the Tramp; Billy West tried it with his 'Candy Kid' (centre left) and was taken to court. He has become a cult figure – note the statuette Zecca is admiring (centre right), even an inspiration to philatelists, see the card, signed by Chaplin, with cancellation marks 'CHARLIE CHAPLIN BEST EVER'!

And still he goes on . . .

1967
A Countess from Hong Kong

Opposite, Sophia Loren, one of the most sensual stars of the international film world

2 **A Countesss from Hong Kong**
Talking picture. 117 minutes (shot between 17 January and May 1966, and first released in London: January 1967)
Director/Screenplay: Charles Chaplin. Assistant director: Jack Causey. Photography: Arthur Ibbetson (Technicolor). Art Director: Bob Cartwright. Editor: Gordon Hales. Music: Charles Chaplin. Music director and arranger: Lambert Williamson. Producer: Jerome Epstein. Cast: Sophia Loren, Marlon Brando, Sydney Chaplin, Tippi Hedren, Margaret Rutherford, Patrick Cargill, Geraldine Chaplin, Michael Medwin, Oliver Johnston, John Paul, Angela Scoular, Bill Nagy, Angela Pringle, Jenny Bridges, Kevin Manser, Carol Cleveland. And Charles Chaplin, appearing as the steward.

The young and handsome millionaire Ogden Mears is depressed by his life. When his ship calls at Hong Kong he meets Natascha, a beautiful Russian woman who claims to be a countess. After the ship has sailed, he discovers that she has stowed away in his stateroom. Torn between his diplomatic career, his estranged wife and Natascha, he opts in the end for life with his countess.

Although he knew it might be his last screen role, Chaplin chose to make only a fleeting appearance in this film. In his directorial role (above) he was considerably more expansive . . .

A Countess from Hong Kong

Chaplin's preparations were as meticulous
as those of the 'method' school of actors

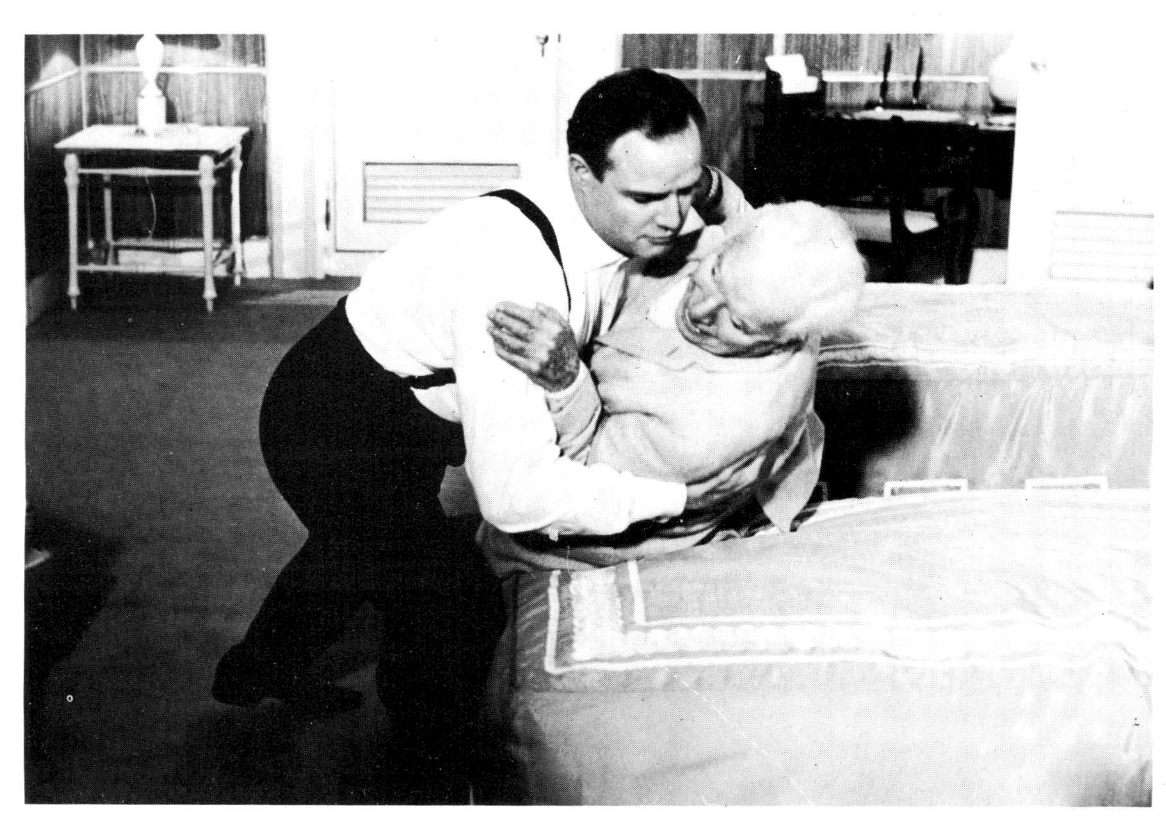

A Countess from Hong Kong

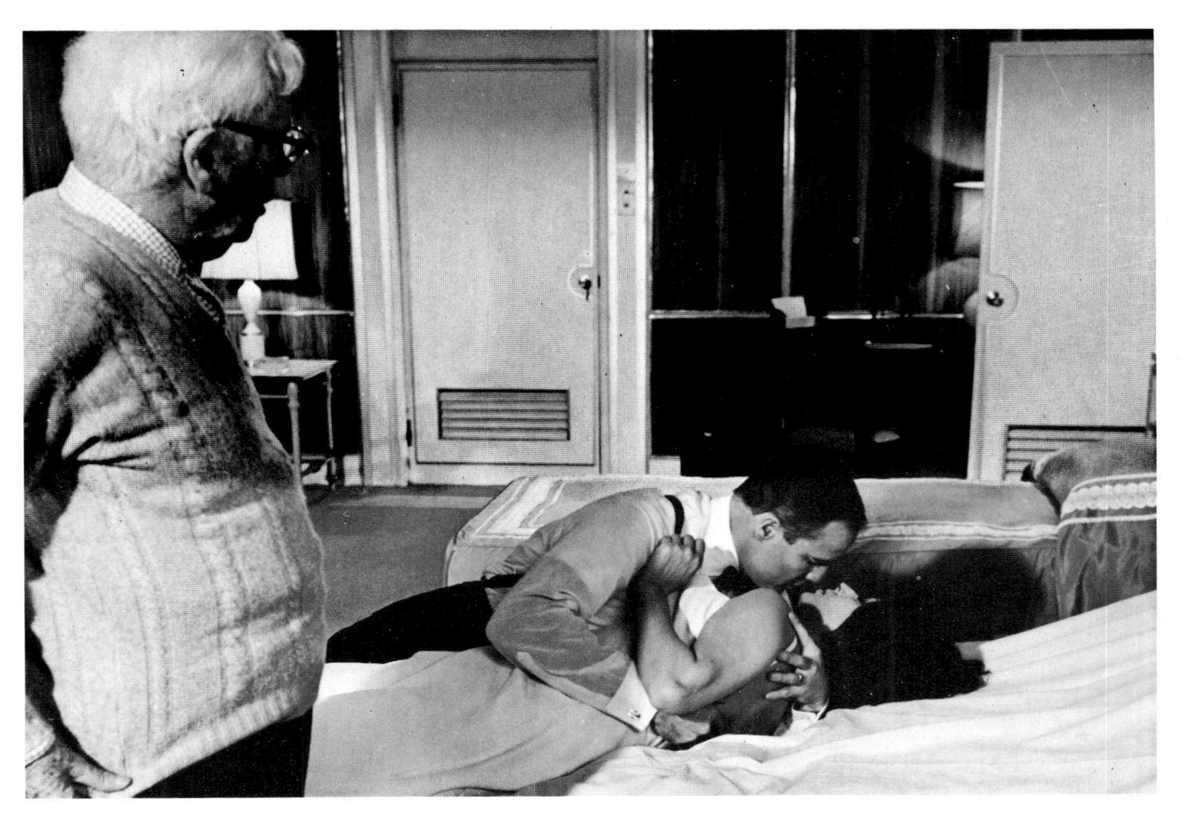

Below, a look of pure devilment from Marlon Brando

A Countess from Hong Kong

Giving direction to his daughter Geraldine

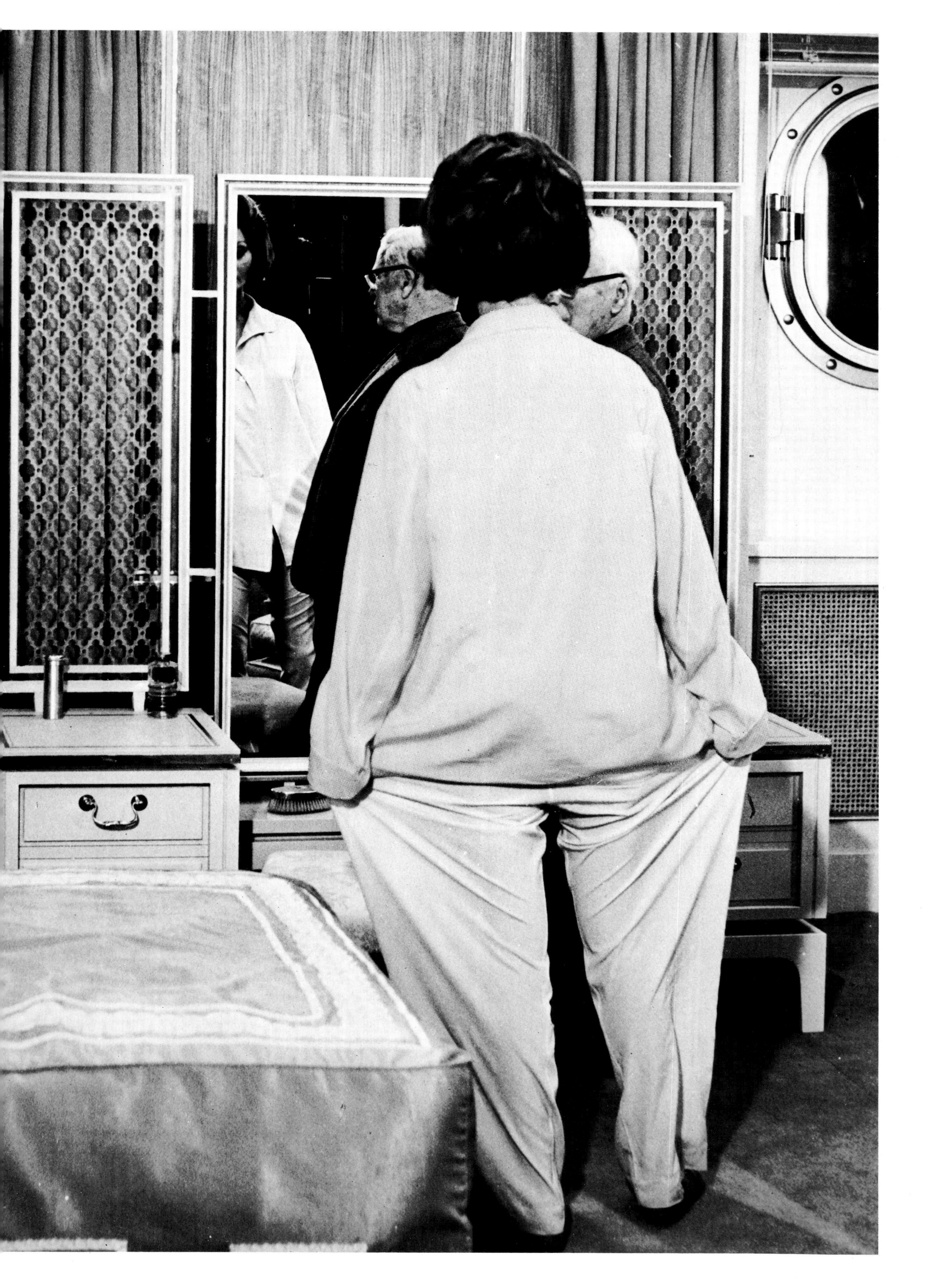

A Countess from Hong Kong

Two faces of the cinema (Sophia Loren and Margaret Rutherford)

A Countess from Hong Kong

With Sydney Chaplin

A private moment with Carlo Ponti . . .

. . . and with the director

 Charles Spencer Chaplin, in Molière's chair

Photo Maurice Zalewski, Paris

Chaplin as seen by J.Cl. Forest, creator of *Barbarella*

Chaplin the Enigma

'I was born', Chaplin tells us in *My Autobiography*, 'on 16th April 1889, at eight o'clock at night, in East Lane, Walworth . . .'

Perhaps that is the literal truth; but various of his biographers, and his son Charles as well, must then be mistaken in claiming that the birth took place at 287 Kennington Road, the house Chaplin revisited when he returned to London in 1921 and again in 1931.

Let us at any rate take it that he was born on 16 April, the son of two vaudeville performers, Charles Chaplin and Hannah Hill, daughter of an Irish cobbler. He had three half-brothers, two of whom achieved recognition: Sydney, older than he, who also became an actor, and Wheeler Dryden, younger, the black sheep of the family (who lived very much in Chaplin's shadow in Hollywood and played bit parts in *Limelight* and *Monsieur Verdoux*).

The father was a heavy drinker who abandoned his wife and son but remained in touch with the family and took over the care of Charles and Sydney for a short period before his death on 10 May 1901, at the age of thirty-seven. The address given by his widow on the death certificate is 16 Golden Place, Chester Street, Lambeth.

It would appear that we have all the information necessary to draw up the family tree of the great Charlie Chaplin, later Sir Charles Chaplin. However, we must remember that most of these facts are supplied by Chaplin himself – not the most reliable informant. In 1922 he declared to friends that he was 'born in a trunk' because his parents were on tour all the time, and that he had therefore spent the first months of his life in the wings of second-rate provincial music-halls. To this day, absolutely no documentary evidence has been found to support either version of the circumstances of his birth. The only official document at our disposal is the death certificate of Sydney Chaplin (dated Nice, 16 April 1965), which was made out in the name of Sydney Hill. Apart from that, there is nothing. The Register of Births and Deaths in London has no record of any Chaplin being born on the day in question.

So we do not know whether Charles came into the world as Chaplin, or as Hill or Hawkes. We may never know.

It is after all conceivable that his baritone father adopted Charles Chaplin as his professional name, just as Hannah Hill took the name of Lily Harley. Almost anything is possible; especially as we know that Charles and Hannah had touring engagements that kept them apart, and that they frequently went their separate ways.

When Chaplin went to the United States in 1910 (via Montreal, so he tells us in his autobiography), passport formalities were not as strictly enforced as they are today. His travelling companion on that occasion was Stan Laurel, whose real name was Arthur Stanley Jefferson. His subsequent employer was Mack Sennett, whose real name was Michael Sinnott; and his co-star Mabel Normand was apparently born Muriel Fortescue. Chaplin's autobiography describes an important moment in the life of the six-year-old boy in the Hanwell School for Orphans and Destitute Children: 'I . . . was taught to write my name, "Chaplin". The word fascinated me and looked like me, I thought.'

When Charles and Sydney entered the Lambeth workhouse with their mother their religion was entered on the admission certificate as 'Protestant'. In later years Charlie Chaplin attended no place of worship. When the Nazis came to power, and gave him a prominent position in their first exhibition 'The Eternal Jew', he made no response. It was a Protestant pastor who blessed the mortal remains of Charles Spencer Chaplin, in the little cemetery of Corsier-sur-Vevey.

In a letter to Arthur Sheekman, dated 5 September 1940, Groucho Marx wrote: 'Last night I had dinner with Chaplin at Dave Chasen's and he was in high humour – unusual for him. He told me among other things that he's not Jewish, but wishes he were. He said he is part Scotch, English and Gypsy, but I think he is not quite sure what he is.'

We have Chaplin's own account of the poverty and hardships of his early life, the failure of his mother's health and her lapses into insanity. Yet in all likelihood Chaplin has done no more than scratch the surface of his childhood. He describes how he joined a clog-dance troupe called the Eight Lancashire Lads at the tender age of nine. At eleven he appeared at the London Hippodrome. The rare occasions when he played with friends in the poor London streets were later recalled as golden times. He never forgot the run-down area of the city where he had snatched whatever pleasures were available. For him, childhood held all the charms of a world he was no longer able to enter. He had a profound need for these streets and this locality, which he was to return to even after an interval of thirty years.

While H.G. Wells, Winston Churchill and George Bernard Shaw were competing for the pleasure of their illustrious visitor's company, he chose to go and see a blind old man who still walked along the same stretch of grimy pavement. He asked him when his dog had died.

'I was right here in the midst of my youth,' he said, 'but somehow I seemed apart from it. I felt as though I was viewing it under a glass. It could be seen all too plainly, but when I reached to touch it it was not there – only the glass could be felt, this glass that had been glazed by the years since I left.'

There followed small parts, tours, hard times. In 1907 he was taken on as a member of Fred Karno's company, where he did a whole series of comedy sketches with Stan Laurel. The troupe went to Paris and played at the Folies-Bergère in 1909. Chaplin talked to Robert Florey 'of the small hotels where he stayed, his meeting with Debussy, his enchantment at seeing Paris by night, and of his various adventures everywhere from Montmartre to the Latin Quarter'.

In 1921 Charlie brought his mother over to Hollywood. She was always smiling and singing under her breath, spoke only rarely and would address invisible animals and butterflies in the gardens of the studio.

For all that we know about the background and origins and religious persuasion of one of the greatest men of this century, there is much that is shadowy supposition, perhaps deliberate mystification. Chaplin encouraged the confusion, for example by telling people that he was born in Fontainebleau, and claiming to remember things he had in fact seen on a brief visit to Paris. His identity was to be his own true creation. '. . . "Chaplin". The word fascinated me and looked like me, I thought . . .'

Chaplin by Marc Chagall

Hollywood: The Golden Years

In 1910 Karno's company went to New York. Chaplin topped the vaudeville bill at the Colonial Theatre. There was a tour of the USA. At the end of the summer of 1913, back again in New York, Chaplin appeared in a sketch called *A Night in an English Music Hall*. He was seen by Adam Kessel, an associate of Thomas Ince and Mack Sennett and one of the owners of the Keystone Comedy Film company; he was sufficiently impressed by the young comedian to ask Karno's manager to release him, so that he could go to California. Chaplin refused at first. He was happy with his friends. But the offer of $150 a week helped him to change his mind. This was to be the start of a meteoric rise to fame.

Yet Mack Sennett was not convinced about his new employee. He asked several directors to try him out but nothing came of it. People said the newcomer didn't have the impact – didn't have a feeling for burlesque. Chaplin began to wonder if he was going to last very long in Hollywood. Then someone did notice him. He was called Henry Lehrman. Of Austrian origin, he was a former streetcar motorman who had broken into films by pretending he was a representative of Pathé Brothers in Paris. He was henceforth known to everyone as Henry 'Pathé' Lehrman.

It was he who gave Chaplin his début in *Making a Living*, which was shot in four days, in early 1914.

'What shall I get him to wear?' he asked Mack Sennett.

'He's English. Dress him up like a lord and give him a pair of whiskers.'

Chaplin accordingly wore a frock-coat, top hat, spats and a monocle, but not with any particular enthusiasm. For his next film he borrowed the pants belonging to Fatty Arbuckle and Chester Conklin's old shoes, acquiring the rest from the actors with whom he shared a dressing-room. A tuft of crêpe hair glued under his nose and a big safety pin to fasten his jacket completed the ensemble. That is how he appeared in *Kid Auto Races at Venice*.

The year 1914 brought success, but it was also a time for experiment and the introduction of new ideas. The tramp's costume underwent continual modification – the famous jacket and hat nearly ended up being light grey; the cane that was to become his trademark was actually a later substitute for the traditional Sennett mallet; but, above all, the character needed time to evolve. The little fellow was aggressive, caustic, sometimes even violent, not above replacing custard pies with heavy stones or knocking his enemies out – or landing a hefty kick on a pretty woman's behind. The recipient of the kick was Mabel Normand – the same Mabel Normand who starred in *Mabel's Married Life*, in which Charlie vents his anger against her lover on a dummy.

Mack Sennett was by now delighted with the eccentric appearance and curious waddling gait adopted by his protégé. In *Mabel's Strange Predicament*, Chaplin invented the business of hopping on one foot and skidding to a halt, using his cane – a new prop – to keep his balance, while holding his bowler hat on his head with his left hand. The figure of Charlie was beginning to take shape.

Yet Chaplin couldn't wait to free himself of Sennett's influence, disliking both his approach to comedy and his routines. Neatly he sidestepped Sennett's authority.

With rather less tact he outmanoeuvred Mabel Normand, who was meant to be the studio star.

He appeared in thirty-five films in one year. Rushed as they were, these one-reelers, with their flagrant borrowings from Karno comedy sketches, already hinted that Chaplin was interested in something more subtle than gags and burlesque. The twenty-second of his films for Keystone, *The Face on the Bar Room Floor*, tells of the despair of a painter abandoned by his pretty wife; when he meets her again years later she is the mother of a family, fatter, no longer beautiful, and surrounded by children. 'I had a narrow escape there!' exclaims Charlie. Mabel Normand turned the part down flat . . .

By 1915 Chaplin had grown to be a well-known and popular comic actor in the United States. His new employers George K. Spoor and 'Broncho Billy' Anderson, owners of the Essanay company, offered him $100,000 a year and complete artistic control. Aptly enough, his first film for them was entitled *His New Job*.

It was at this time that he met a young secretary of twenty called Edna Purviance, born, charmingly, in Paradise Valley. 'She was more than pretty, she was beautiful,' Charlie wrote in his autobiography. He was instantly attracted to her and she became his close companion and his co-star.

Money, fame, freedom and love had arrived all at once. They were heady days. Chaplin used his new experiences to round out Charlie's screen character, to tone down his quick temper and to introduce a love interest. Of the forty films he made that year, among the best remembered are *Carmen*, a magnificent present to his beloved, and *A Woman*, in which he appeared in drag, causing the film to be banned in several countries.

1915 was also the year of *The Tramp*, in which the pathos of the legendary figure emerged for the first time; who can forget him sitting on the grass in the countryside, cleaning his nails before he eats his meagre little snack?

In 1916 Mutual Films offered him $650,000 (and in the event he received more) for making twelve two-reelers; the series was shot between March 1916 and July 1917. This sequence of more carefully made and better constructed films includes some unforgettable masterpieces: *One A.M.*, a solo performance in which the star's only partners are objects; *Easy Street*, which contains the famous joke of the tough guy's head being trapped inside the gas streetlamp; and *The Immigrant*, a classic – as indeed, on reflection, are the other nine.

1918: Chaplin was twenty-nine. Eight of the films he was to make for First National (for which he was given a contract worth a million dollars) would be feature-length. It is enough merely to mention their titles: *A Dog's Life*, *Shoulder Arms*, *Sunnyside*, *A Day's Pleasure*, *The Idle Class*, *Pay Day* and *The Pilgrim*, his last film with Edna Purviance, and of course, *The Kid*.

He contracted a hasty marriage with Mildred Harris. She later bore him a child who died at birth. 'A poor little thing who didn't even have time to smile,' was Chaplin's reaction. Without further ado he obtained a divorce. His mood darkened following this abortive venture into matrimony. Then one day, his mind wandering aimlessly, he stumbled on the idea for *The Kid*. In shooting this, he created the self he would like to have been. Since it is impossible

Chaplin by André Lhote

to turn the clock back in reality, he used his art to fabricate a childhood, asking a boy actor to be the incarnation of himself as a child. Jackie Coogan somehow took on Charlie's mannerisms, his expressions and his looks.

It is no coincidence that *The Kid* was Chaplin's first film drama. Equally it is no coincidence that he emerged from the production in a state of collapse, suffering from nervous exhaustion.

One morning, although he was in the middle of shooting *The Idle Class*, he simply left Hollywood without telling anyone and sailed for England. There he attended the première of *The Kid* in the only city that had a sentimental importance for him in the context of that film: London.

Fame

Chaplin by Jean Epstein

Chaplin's fame was by now world-wide. The US Government asked him to take part in the campaign to raise funds for the war effort. With Douglas Fairbanks and Mary Pickford, he addressed public meetings, and made his first propaganda film, *The Bond* (1918).

Chaplin decided the time had come to form an independent company and to build his own studio, where he would be able to work in peace and take all the time he needed. He chose a site on La Brea Avenue, in the heart of Hollywood. To celebrate the opening, Chaplin solemnly put on Charlie's famous big shoes and marked his footprints in the wet cement at the entrance to the set where he was to shoot his greatest films; with the tip of his cane, he signed his name and wrote the date on which the building was completed: 21 January 1918.

I visited the studios in 1938. Alf Reeves, who took me round, warned me in advance:

'Our studio is the only one in Hollywood that isn't wired for sound. You can't use it for talkies!'

In his company I relived a whole host of sad memories . . .

Chaplin was never exactly open-handed with money and his films were always produced on a shoestring. The sets were tatty, dilapidated, old painted flats; I discovered that the swimming pool where the drowning in *City Lights* was shot was not much more than a ditch; and there was 'the street', always the same in all his films, the shop on the corner becoming a florist's in *City Lights*, a drugstore in *Modern Times*. An air of neglect hung over it all. The wooden panels were crumbling away, the paint was flaking. The refuse-bin was old and dented. The old dog that was the studio mascot could hardly stand on its four legs, and lived in a battered kennel.

Chaplin let me see his dressing-room. Not in the least luxurious, it had a functional bathroom and kitchenette attached. A few odd glasses stood by an empty carafe. On the table, tubes and pots of theatrical make-up, years old. A few traces of cream inside the jars, the tubes squeezed almost dry, their contents hard and powdery. In a cupboard hung some of Charlie's costumes, threadbare frock-coats, the overalls from *Modern Times*, stinking of oil, and one battered, faded bowler hat. Dressing-rooms in provincial theatres have better mirrors than the small piece of distorting glass before which Chaplin applied his make-up.

Poverty fitted Charlie like a glove. You could feel it everywhere. Even in the office where he wrote his last script with a scratchy old fountain pen (to which I helped myself as a souvenir!).

Only one surprise: the female star's dressing-room. This was created for Edna Purviance and was subsequently used by Charlie's many co-stars and lovers. The current occupant, Paulette Goddard, had fitted it out with a degree of modest luxury, scattering about portraits of herself and her mother and sketches of Mickey Mouse and Donald Duck signed and dedicated by Walt Disney. Ravishingly lovely photographs of Paulette were to be seen all over the studios, standing out among the yellowing documents and old-fashioned caricatures that still hung in their original positions.

'It's just a small studio,' Chaplin said to me later. 'Really quite small, but it's enough for one man.'

In 1919 Chaplin had founded United Artists in association with Mary Pickford, Douglas Fairbanks and another Hollywood 'great', the director D.W. Griffith.

At this period Chaplin and the French comic Max Linder were neighbours and used to meet quite often. Linder introduced him to a young French journalist called Robert Florey, who was in the habit of bringing him French film magazines, articles by Louis Delluc and so forth; Chaplin came across Florey again at the Fairbanks' house, where he was a regular visitor, using the pool and partnering his host at badminton. He took a great liking to the young man, allowing him to come and go as he wished at the studio and taking him to lunch at places like Musso Frank's or the Gotham. Although Florey started a new career as a film director, he never lost his journalistic instincts, and noted down, and later published, everything he knew about Chaplin, his friends, opinions and projects. Consequently we have a fair amount of information about the Chaplin of the period from *The Pilgrim* to *Monsieur Verdoux*.

After *The Kid* opened in London, Charlie toured Europe in triumph. In Paris, crowds thronged the Gare Saint-Lazare and then flocked to the Place de la Concorde to gather outside the Crillon. Chaplin responded to the cheers by appearing on the hotel balcony. To everyone's amusement he was awarded a minor decoration by Léon Bérard, Minister for Public Instruction – being created an Officier de l'Instruction Publique. In Berlin he met Pola Negri, a Polish film star at the height of her career; they exchanged compliments and looked deep into each other's eyes. Pola was twenty-three, a little old for Chaplin's taste, but there was no denying her attraction.

Then back to Hollywood to finish *The Pilgrim*, which called down on his head the wrath of puritanical American society. Really, this clown was going too far. Wasn't he a dangerous revolutionary? Pola Negri arrived in Hollywood. The press seized on the event. This would be the wedding of the century. Chaplin felt he should meet her at the station, and suddenly the affair was on. But it was an affair in which publicity played a greater part than love, and it lasted only a few months. Pola later found consolation in the arms of Rudolph Valentino.

Having at last fulfilled his contract with First National, Chaplin was free to launch out on his own. He did not appear in his first film, being content to direct Edna Purviance in the starring role. With its French setting and extravagant melodrama, *A Woman of Paris* was hugely successful – beyond its merits.

A little brunette called Lita Grey had caught Chaplin's eye when she took a small part in *The Kid*. He married her on 24 November 1924. One of her attractions was her extreme youth – she was just sixteen. The Daughters of the American Revolution expressed their disapproval. Lita Grey bore Chaplin two children but she did not in the event play the starring role she had been promised in *The Gold Rush*. This went instead to the gorgeous Georgia Hale. *The Gold Rush*, made in 1924–5, is Chaplin at the height of his powers; in it we experience that laughter mingled with tears that is the essence of his genius, all the pathos of the little fellow with the big heart, sublime in defeat. Genius like that is unanswerable. Supremely confident, it sweeps all before it.

Chaplin's emotional life was in confusion. His faithful friend Edna Purviance had departed. He had made a terrible mistake in marrying Lita Grey, who had literally been pushed into his arms by a domineering mother. He had escaped the threat of being charged with abducting a minor, but now he was trapped.

Backed up by a posse of ferocious lawyers, Lita Grey filed for divorce on grounds of perverted and indecent behaviour. The lawyers invoked article 288 of the Penal Code, which carried a mandatory sentence of fifteen years imprisonment for acts of 'oral copulation'. The press tore into Chaplin. His reputation, his fortune and his freedom were all at stake. The hypocrites and prudes bayed for his blood; the women's leagues launched campaigns against him and spread vicious rumours. All Charlie's funds and assets were frozen. He was a broken man, on the verge of collapse. Only then was it made clear to him that what he was required to do was pay – large sums of money in ready cash. He agreed, paid vast fees to all the lawyers and settled an initial sum of $800,000 on his ex-wife. The affair aged him by twenty years, but in spite of it all he completed *The Circus*, another masterpiece.

The death of his mother was a further ordeal. With her poor health and wandering mind, Hannah was nevertheless the last link with his London childhood. He was stricken with grief. Yet he went on to make the extraordinary *City Lights*.

The first three of Chaplin's 'major' films were love stories, but in all of them it was clear from the start that love would not be returned; the adventurer, the clown and the tramp have no claim to happiness.

When Paulette Goddard arrived on the scene, with all her many charms, love took on a new dimension for the little fellow. He was completely smitten.

The talkies had recently arrived. *City Lights* was a gesture of defiance to the new films that had been so successful in boosting cinema audiences over the past three years. Chaplin declared that he would never talk. He was to keep his word in *Modern Times* but spoke veritable tirades in the film that followed.

Nevertheless the coming of sound gave him pause for thought. Over the next five years he did make certain changes, so that the studio was at least soundproofed even if not up-to-date in other respects. He had a number of ideas for effects that he could use in future films. But he never did wire the studios for sound, being content to hire portable recording equipment whenever he needed it. It was the old story – a penny saved is a penny earned. Between 1931 and 1934 Chaplin was much preoccupied with a long-cherished scheme for a film of *Napoleon*, but then started work on another silent movie, *Modern Times*. His co-star was the ravishingly beautiful actress from Sam Goldwyn's company, Paulette Goddard. Unfortunately, audiences were at a loss to know why they were not allowed to hear what the actors were saying to each other.

I met Chaplin in Beverly Hills. He was a disappointed man, on edge and bitter.

'*Modern Times* showed me that it's pointless to try and repeat yourself.'

He talked of the old days with Essanay, said how heartbroken he was at the divorce of Fairbanks and Pickford, his very old friends, and discussed the projects he was working on.

'I wrote three scripts for Paulette and me. Then I tore them up and started again. I don't think I'll ever wear my tramp costume again. Any more than I'll ever make a *Napoleon* . . . Who can say, perhaps one day I'll find a character who is completely different from the one I've got used to. Then I'll talk. I've abandoned *The Wild Woman of Bali*, but I've still promised Paulette a script, which I'll direct. In the meantime she's working with Selznick . . .

'My autobiography? Of course I want to write it, but I don't know where to begin . . .'

Then suddenly the one sentence of French that he knew – he'd learned it from a Linguaphone record and had been producing it at intervals for the last twenty years.

'*Bonjour, je vais prendre le train à la gare!*' (Good day, I'm going to catch the train at the station.)

He went on to discuss the international situation, the wars that were brewing. But clearly something was very wrong. It seems cruel that genius is so invariably a prey to these harrowing afflictions of the spirit.

He toyed with his cane and suddenly held it out to me.

'Here you are, take my stick, Charlie the Tramp is dead and I don't need it any more.'

Chaplin by Paul Colin

Chaplin by Frans Masereel

Infamy

Chaplin married Paulette Goddard during a visit to the Far East in the first half of 1936. They were blissfully happy together, travelled extensively and entertained a lot. Paulette was to be his leading lady in *The Great Dictator* but she was not to be his last wife. They were divorced in 1942, and Paulette was awarded a million-dollar settlement.

Once again Chaplin was caught in a legal battle with yet another young woman, Joan Barry. She filed a paternity suit against him and dredged up a forgotten statute originally introduced to stop the white slave trade. Again there was much scandal and muck-raking, a systematic campaign of vilification in which religion, politics, chauvinist attitudes and tax arrears all played a part. Again Chaplin had to dig deep into his pocket in order to be left in peace. He had his revenge in *Monsieur Verdoux* – donning a well-cut suit instead of the usual shabby tramp's outfit. The original script idea was supplied by Orson Welles and, as the film was set in Paris, Chaplin engaged Robert Florey as his co-director.

He put aside the messianic outpourings of *The Great Dictator*, the departure of Paulette and his recent marriage to Oona O'Neill, and allowed his latent misogyny to erupt: woman was the eternal enemy, she had to be killed, and not just one woman, all women. Hence *Monsieur Verdoux*.

Inevitably, there was an outcry.

All America regretted it had ever said it loved Charlie. He was a dirty foreigner. A leftie? Perhaps a Jew? He was castigated for his taste for young women, his many divorces, his lawsuits.

And now this disgusting film.

He was deeply wounded, a profoundly depressed and saddened man, when I met him at his home in Summit Drive.

As I walked through the bright drawing-room I caught sight of Chaplin's head, just his head with its thatch of white hair, in a glass cage formed by the verandah. Aware that it was no more than an optical illusion and another couple of steps would dispel the frightening vision, I stopped for a moment to look at the head divorced from its body, the face impassive, waxily pale and with a wide-eyed devouring gaze. But as I approached, my host's features were lit up by an angelic smile. Heavens, this great man is such an endearing fellow! Every time I met him I thought the same thing. He was very much off-duty, darting about in old clothes that were too small for him: beige jacket, white trousers, frayed pullover and worn tennis shoes. He was one of those men who take a long time to get used to clothes and then can never bear to throw them away.

There he was, wrinkled now, his hands covered in freckles, his magnificent white hair still as curly as a child's, directing at me that devastating smile of his, a blend of god-like benevolence and roguish charm – the look of a fallen archangel. Those eyes blotted out everything else, you were held by them, fascinated, they pierced straight to the heart. You felt they had the power to examine consciences. They moved from laughter to tears, then went blank. What was it, I wondered, that gave them that expressive power, that intensity? And I suddenly realized they were the eyes of forgiveness. A man full of imperfections as well as great brilliance. A great man, good and kind and peace-loving, and underneath it all still the little fellow of the Charlie Chaplin films.

So why had he abandoned the character?

'I had to make *Monsieur Verdoux*. I had to throw myself into this attack on the nature of man, attempt a satire on human frailty. I wanted to prove that humour isn't just a matter of jokes, it can't exist without a social dimension. Do you remember Swift saying that the children of the poor served no purpose and they should be used for food? I went even further, and in the scene where the girl is poisoned I want people to be aware of the sadism. Is it my fault that the Americans are incapable of feeling anything? I thought they'd be shocked at first, but then they'd discover the key to understanding a character who can't cope with his life and becomes a victim of circumstances. The real criminal isn't Verdoux, it's life itself, the world about him, society.'

Chaplin clenched his fists.

'What really upsets them, you see, is that Monsieur Verdoux is a little bourgeois, an ordinary little man just like them, a poor fellow who has lost his job and has a family to keep.

'Monsieur Verdoux knows life is a struggle. He has to look after his own. And so, he sets about it with the same clearsightedness as the GI who has been told that the best way to protect his family is to use a flame-thrower with maximum efficiency.

'That didn't go down very well with *them*. The press went for me. There's one lawsuit after another. They want to cut me down to size, terrorize me. I know they're going to haul me off to Washington to appear before the Un-American Activities Committee, they'll threaten to deport me. But I'll go there with my head held high. I know how to speak, I can defend myself when I'm attacked. I'll tell them exactly what I think. I won't mince my words. My arguments are good ones, and I've got right on my side. I'll make them listen.'

He clutched at the arm of the couch.

'They want me dead, but they won't succeed.'

I spoke to him about Europe and France. I told him how high his reputation was in France, how greatly he was loved and respected. I explained to him how students used to turn up in their hundreds, during the Occupation, running the most appalling risks just to see one of his films.

'It would be a sign of weakness for me to leave. Of course I should like to go to Europe, to France especially, to the South. But I'm an old man. I'm nearly sixty. I've worked here all my life. I love my dear house, my good old studios, where no one but me can work. I dare not leave this cruel place, where even a great man like Griffith wasn't appreciated. You think you're going to find monuments and universities and museums in Hollywood, but all people think of is opening new restaurants.'

'What will happen to Hollywood, do you think?'

'There's the money and there's the work. That's what it boils down to. Up till now it's the money that's been important, but you can't rely on it all coming good any more, just because the money's there. Now it's the work that matters, and that's a threat that weighs heavily on Hollywood the golden. All those films on which they spend such fortunes, they're all alike. Just the same old script, over and over again.'

He brushed away a tear, then:

'I'm tired and I'm fed up, I can't stand it . . .'

Suddenly he launched himself at me, grabbed me by the lapels and cried out:

'You're right! What does it matter if this bunch of creeps don't like me, as long as I give something to other people . . . You give me new strength by offering the friendship of the French people. I'll show them I'm not finished.'

He slumped back exhausted.

'I'm nothing, nothing special. But I'm going to carry on saying what I've got to say. I shall go on being a pacifist and I'll speak out against this new war that people seem to want.

'You should be spared that. I know what France has gone through. I can understand where these new philosophies come from, in your country, though some people find it all too easy to dismiss them. Man turning inward, looking for consolation within himself, it comes from those years of suffering.'

Abruptly he changed tack.

'You make some excellent films. The day I saw that extraordinary *Blood of a Poet*, I knew that from now on Hollywood would have to take notice of France.'

Then suddenly, full of enthusiasm:

'I worked very hard on *Monsieur Verdoux*. I threw it in their faces. And I'll go on rubbing their noses in their own folly. I've got an idea for a story about a clown. . . . And a film about American life,

Washington, the press. . . . I didn't go back to my character of Charlie the Tramp because we're all in a ghastly mess and I felt I had something else to say. But I'll bring the little fellow back, with his baggy pants, I'll bring back pantomime. Mind you, the Americans don't understand Charlie either, because they don't know what suffering is.'

I tried to change the subject.

'Charlie, your love life has often raised a storm in the press, women have caused you a good deal of pain, what are your feelings now?'

An unforgettable smile lit up his whole face. He stood up and exclaimed joyfully:

'I've found happiness, true happiness. It took a long time and it's not been easy. But I am happy, completely happy. I adore all my children and I think they love me.'

In the space of a few seconds he was transformed, suddenly rejuvenated. We went for a walk on the lawn. We had tea together and came within an ace of throwing jam tarts in each other's faces.

'Come on,' he said, 'I'd like to play for you.'

And the great Chaplin sat down at his Steinway and played me a selection of the music from *Monsieur Verdoux*, original score by Charles Chaplin.

Chaplin by Fernand Léger

J. Cl. Forest

Gentleman and Tramp

Chaplin had certain peculiarities that are of interest in forming an understanding of his character. He was left-handed. We all know the famous photo of the tramp playing a miniature violin – and Chaplin did indeed learn to play the instrument. But for a man who is left-handed that poses all kinds of problems. Chaplin anyway experienced difficulty in telling left from right. When he was looking through a camera lens his confusion was compounded.

The actor Jack Oakie (who played the part of Napaloni in *The Great Dictator*, and always regretted he was not called Benzino Gasolino as in the original script) has given an amusing account of Chaplin's anger with a young bit-player who was supposed to bring in a dish of food, but who seemed incapable of reproducing the move he had asked for. The dispute was only resolved when Oakie passed on a message to the exasperated director, explaining that the actress was instinctively using her right hand for a gesture Chaplin performed with his left.

A second peculiarity, and one which has aroused more comment, has to do with Chaplin's sexual preferences, and in particular his obsession with very young women. In a country where the abduction of a minor carried a heavy penalty, such a predilection could only be legitimized by marriage. Chaplin made Mildred Harris his wife when she was sixteen; Lita Grey was also sixteen; Paulette Goddard, at twenty-four, was the exception; and Oona, his last wife and now his widow, was eighteen at the time of their marriage. It is surprising that this preference did not surface in the films, where the beloved – most frequently Edna Purviance – was a mature woman of obvious attractions.

Chaplin's relationships were passionate, tempestuous – and of short duration.

'With Chaplin,' said Florey, 'things just broke up or faded away, like a storm in late summer.'

Women cast a spell over him. Why could he not stay with them?

The Tramp of the films was always reaching for the impossible dream, destroying himself and others in the process; he knew that women were potent and dangerous creatures. Did this, perhaps, reflect something of the nature of this creator: a man who wanted to be Faust but ended by behaving like Don Juan?

Fortunately for him, fate took a hand. His last wife, young and delightful, brought him a happy old age. He was fortunate in finding an exceptional woman.

There is an intriguing and little-known story that relates to these events. It was at the time when Orson Welles was the golden boy of Hollywood. He used to entertain his friends with superb displays of magic, all the more impressive as he had an uncanny ability to predict the future. A famous playwright of his acquaintance asked him to act as his young daughter's escort for an evening, since she wanted to visit a nightclub for the first time. Orson played the part of the gallant host, and at the end of the evening offered to tell the girl's fortune by reading the palm of her hand.

'It's strange,' he concluded, 'you'll marry very young . . . Quite soon . . . And I can even reveal your husband's name. It's Charlie Chaplin.'

The girl blushed and burst out laughing. It was Oona O'Neill.

Also of considerable interest is Chaplin's choice of subject matter for his films. The figure of the tramp – an unemployed scrounger of no fixed address – necessarily defined the figure of his enemy, the policeman or cop who stood for order, morality and the protection of private property. Chaplin used this archetypal confrontation to maximum effect, extracting from it every ounce of humour. But he also had two other principal sources of inspiration, which provided him with some wonderful virtuoso moments: fantasy and dance. Sometimes the two were combined, as in *Sunnyside*, *The Kid* and *The Gold Rush*. Fantasy is a significant element in *His Prehistoric Past*, *The Bank*, *The Kid*, *Shoulder Arms* and *Limelight*.

Dance plays a small part in *The Knock Out* and *The Rounders*, and figures prominently in *Dough and Dynamite*, *Tillie's Punctured Romance*, *Behind the Screen*, *The Rink*, *City Lights*, *Modern Times* and *The Great Dictator*.

Another recurrent motif is that of the double or look-alike (*A Night in the Show*, *The Floorwalker* and *The Great Dictator*) and of the man disguised as a woman (*A Busy Day*, *The Masquerader* and *A Woman*).

The theme of a man trying to cope with recalcitrant objects is a running gag that is used in practically all of the films, the *tour de force* being the solo performance *One A.M.*

As the films show, in some cases to their detriment, Chaplin had little interest in technique, indeed he despised it. But we should bear in mind that, right from the early days with Keystone, he was allowed to edit his own films – something that was quite unheard-of. And his ability as an editor – at a time when no such expertise existed – is quite astonishing.

Jean Mitry has rightly pointed out that the little fellow was not actually a tramp at all but 'a man who has come down in the world, an unfortunate who is looking for work or hoping something will turn up, still aspiring to elegance in his dirty old clothes'.

Of course this character was only arrived at by a process of trial and error. Charlie tried his hand at every job under the sun: pedlar, film-extra, waiter, pavement-layer, bandit, boxing referee, dentist, props man, painter, film actor, nurse, janitor, baker, removal man, and many more. From time to time he would pop up again in his original incarnation as a dandy (in *Making a Living*). Thus we have the wealthy man-about-town of *Cruel, Cruel Love*, the drunken reveller of *The Rounders*, the city gent of *Tillie's Punctured Romance*, the man on a spree in *A Night Out*, the fake aristocrat of *A Jitney*

Elopement, the dress-suited hero of *A Night in the Show* and *One A.M.*, and the boatered spa-visitor of *The Cure*.

The world-famous little fellow, who doesn't know whether to laugh or cry, makes his first appearance in *The Champion*, followed by *In the Park*, *The Tramp*, *The Vagabond* and *Easy Street*. The character reaches a significant stage of development in *The Immigrant* and is fully formed in *A Dog's Life*, made in 1918. His illustrious career came to an abrupt end when Chaplin made *The Great Dictator*, at the age of fifty.

The date 16 June 1943 marked the beginning of a new and happier era in the life of Charles Spencer Chaplin, British citizen. At the age of fifty-four he married Oona O'Neill, aged eighteen. In July 1944 his daughter Geraldine was born. Events moved rapidly. *Limelight* was an enormous success; the Chaplins left the United States and settled in Switzerland; Oona took British nationality. There were more children, and an extremely happy family life. Chaplin made two more films to keep his hand in (*A King in New York* and *A Countess from Hong Kong*), both shot in Britain, and he received a knighthood. Somewhat shamefacedly, Hollywood eventually awarded him a special Oscar, in 1972, and Charlie returned for a few hours to the town that owed so much to him. People were astonished to see that he had become an old man who had difficulty in walking, a chubby-faced white-haired gentleman, wrapped in a heavy overcoat, who spoke slowly and with an effort.

His studio had disappeared, replaced by a supermarket and a record company. The chair he had sat in for over thirty years had been carted away for a few dollars.

Charlie Chaplin, the genius who had made the whole world laugh, died in December 1977, on Christmas night, at the age of eighty-eight.

At the Ritz Hotel, 1971
Chaplin looks at the walking-stick he used in *Modern Times*, which he gave me in Hollywood

Chronology

Index of Titles

Acknowledgments

'The great poet Charles Chaplin',
drawing by Jean Cocteau

Chronology

1889 16 April, birth of Charles Spencer Chaplin in London.
1894 First (impromptu) stage appearance at a variety theatre at Aldershot after his mother's voice failed and she was forced to leave the stage.
1894–8 Years of poverty.
1898 Joins the Eight Lancashire Lads, a clog-dance troupe.
1901 Death of his father, Charles Chaplin senior.
1907 Joins Fred Karno's comedy company.
1910 New York with Karno company. Tour of USA.
1913 Hollywood. Chaplin joins Mack Sennett's studio (15 December).
1914 First film: *Making a Living* (2 February).
Second film: *Kid Auto Races at Venice* (7 February).
Third film: *Mabel's Strange Predicament* (9 February); Mabel Normand is his co-star.
Chaplin is paid $10,000 for his 35 films with Keystone.
1915 Under contract to Essanay (14 films).
Appearance of Edna Purviance in the second Essanay film (*A Night Out*).
Chaplin is paid $60,000 for his 14 films for Essanay.
1916 Under contract to Mutual (12 films). Chaplin is paid $670,000.
1917 Under contract to First National (8 feature films). Chaplin is paid a million dollars.
1918 Opening of Chaplin's studio in Hollywood.
Marries Mildred Harris (aged sixteen).
1919 Founding of United Artists.
Begins shooting *The Kid* (released 1921); Lita Grey appears in a small part.
1920 Divorce from Mildred Harris.
1921 Berlin. Meeting with Pola Negri.
1922 Begins shooting *The Pilgrim* (released 1923; last appearance by Edna Purviance in a film as co-actor with Chaplin).
Engaged to Pola Negri.
Begins shooting *A Woman of Paris* (directed but not performed in by Chaplin; released 1923) with Edna Purviance.
1923 End of engagement to Pola Negri.
1924 Begins shooting *The Gold Rush* with Georgia Hale (released 1925).
Marries Lita Grey (aged sixteen).
1925 Begins shooting *The Circus* with Merna Kennedy (released 1928).
1927 Divorce from Lita Grey.

1928 Begins shooting *City Lights* with Virginia Cherrill (released 1931).
1931 Trip to France. Romance with May Reeves.
1934 Begins shooting *Modern Times* with Paulette Goddard (released 1936).
1936 Marries Paulette Goddard.
1939 Begins shooting *The Great Dictator* with Paulette Goddard (released 1940).
1942 Divorce from Paulette Goddard.
1943 Marries Oona O'Neill (aged eighteen).
1944 Birth of Geraldine.
1946 Shoots *Monsieur Verdoux* (released in the same year).
1947 Press campaign against Chaplin for 'un-American activities'.
1951 Begins shooting *Limelight* (released 1952).
1952 Final departure from the United States.
1953 Move to a permanent home in Switzerland.
1954 Oona granted British citizenship.
1957 Shoots *A King in New York* (released in the same year).
1958 Death of Edna Purviance.
1964 Publication of *My Autobiography*, in London.
1965 Death of his elder half-brother Sydney Chaplin.
1972 Return to Hollywood for a Special Academy Award.
1975 Receives a knighthood.
The Gentleman Tramp: the Chaplins at Vevey.
1977 Death of Chaplin (24–25 December).
Chaplin was buried in the cemetery of Corsier-sur-Vevey.
His remains were stolen from the grave on 2 March 1978, and were recovered at Noville on 17 May.

Index of Titles

Original titles are in capitals. Titles of re-releases are in italics

Photo P. Slade, Paris-Match.

Acknowledgments

The author's gratitude is due to the late Robert Florey, to Simon Dargols and to Rachel Ford; and also to those who assisted him in completing his collection of material: Claude Beylie, Charles Ford, Jacques Itah, Pierre Leprohon, Pierre Lherminier, André Marinie, J. Michaux-Bellaire, Jean Mitry, Roger Thérond (*Paris-Match*), Maurice Zalewski.

PITTSBURGH FILMMAKERS
477 MELWOOD AVENUE
PITTSBURGH, PA 15213

PITTSBURGH FILMMAKERS
477 MELWOOD AVENUE
PITTSBURGH, PA 15213